Stoicism & Western Buddhism:

A Reflection on Two Philosophical Ways of Life

Patrick Ussher

First published in 2018

This work is copyright © Patrick John Redmond Ussher.

Cover design by Rocio De Torres Artillo
(www.rociodetorres.com)

About the Author

Patrick Ussher was a member of the *Stoicism Today* project from its inception in 2012 until 2016, a collaboration of academics and psychotherapists which provides modernised Stoic resources, based on the ancient Greco-Roman philosophy as a way of life. Patrick contributed to the development of three 'International Stoic Weeks' (2012-2014), which were widely featured in the media including on BBC Radio, and in newspapers such as *The Guardian*, *Forbes* and *The Telegraph*. Patrick founded and edited the blog for the *Stoicism Today* project and has edited two books *Stoicism Today: Selected Writings (Volumes One & Two)*.

Patrick has also written *POTS: What It Really Is & Why It Happens*, a book which argues for a neurological cause to the condition Postural Orthostatic Tachycardia Syndrome (POTS) following an antecedent trauma, such as a viral illness, surgery, pregnancy or psychological trauma (or a combination).

Patrick has a BA and MA in Classics from the University of Exeter, U.K. He lives in Dublin, Ireland.

Contents

Preface i
Introduction: The Modern-Day Revival of Buddhism
and of Stoicism 1
Chapter One: A Similar Spirit 31
Chapter Two: Mindfulness in Stoicism & Buddhism ... 50
Chapter Three: Cultivating Compassion 72
Conclusion 90
Bibliography 101

Preface

In 2012, I wrote a dissertation as part of my MA in Classics at the University of Exeter which compared Stoicism, the ancient Greco-Roman philosophy as a way of life, with Buddhism as practised in the West. This dissertation was written before the formation of the *Stoicism Today* project in October 2012, of which I was then a member for four years, founding and editing the *Stoicism Today* blog and taking part in compiling resources for the annual International 'Stoic Week'. The *Stoicism Today* project is now also known as the *Modern Stoicism* project and more information about it can be found here: http://modernstoicism.com.

I decided to return to my MA thesis and rework it so as to be suitable for publication as a short book for a more general audience, although the work does still necessarily retain a quasi-academic style and structure. The book is best thought of as a kind of extended, reflective essay. I hope that it will be of interest and of help to those seeking to practice a combination of Stoicism and Buddhism in their own lives and that it will also be a catalyst for reflection on the nature of the ongoing 'reinvention' of both Stoicism and Buddhism in their current forms.

Patrick Ussher
Dublin, February 2018.

Introduction

The Modern-Day Revival of Buddhism and of Stoicism[1]

Many modern Stoics also follow a Buddhist or Buddhist-derived meditation practice. Many Stoics, indeed, find the two approaches to be complementary. On the other hand, many modern-day Buddhists, upon encountering Stoic philosophy through a Buddhist lens, are struck by the parallels with their own approach. But why should this be the case?

For the person who is unfamiliar with modern Stoic or modern Buddhist practice, but who just has a sense of their classical forms, the two philosophies do not, at first glance, appear to have much in common. On the one hand, in the Greco-Roman philosophy of Stoicism we have a philosophical way of life embedded within a theistic worldview. On the other hand, in classical Buddhism, we have an atheistic yet religious philosophy focussed on attaining a positive future rebirth along with a monastic emphasis on asceticism.

---

[1] A short note on the footnotes in this book: regarding original sources, I note the author, the ancient text and the location of the source (e.g. Epictetus, *Discourses,* 1.3.4). For secondary sources, I note the year of the book's publication and page reference (e.g. 1997, 8). From the *Bibliography* at the end of this book, you can then find the full title of the book cited and other bibliographical information.

Why should these two different world-views complement each other? Why does a modern Stoic also look to practise Buddhist vipassana or insight meditation and find that this enhances, rather than diminishes, his own practice of Stoic virtue?

The answer lies in how we in the modern world have reinterpreted and continue to reinterpret both traditions in light of our own needs in the modern age. Strange as it may seem, the Buddhism that most Westerners (or those of a Western mindset) practise today is not the same as the Buddhism of the Buddha and, likewise, the Stoicism of many modern-day Stoics is not the same as that of the original Stoa. And yet the subsequent modern 'reinventions' of both philosophies are far more similar to each other than their respective ancient forms ever were.

In this book, I aim to explore, first of all, the nature of the reinvention of both systems: why do we in the modern world need to change the original forms of these philosophies and what does this say about *us*? In what ways have we changed Stoicism and Buddhism: which parts do we leave out and which do we emphasise, and why? And then, in the main part of the book, I aim to set out the core similarities which these philosophies share, in such a way that aims to be helpful to those who are seeking to practise a combination of both philosophies in their lives. Finally, I conclude with further reflections on the ongoing adaptations of both philosophies and on how each philosophy might positively inform the other.

Developing 'Western' Buddhism

An idea often associated with mindfulness in its most straightforward forms is to 'live in the present'. However, many modern-day Buddhists would be surprised to learn that this idea was not something that the Buddha himself ever suggested. Not once in the entire corpus of the Pali Canon (the oldest collections of teachings attributed to the Buddha) does he mention the present moment, and he certainly did not talk about deliberately enjoying or savouring it.[2] But, then again, the original Buddhist texts are not read too often by Western Buddhists. If they were to read them, they might come across such passages as the following:

> 'What there is with regard to form, feeling, ideas, activity and consciousness, he (the monk) regards these things as impermanent, as suffering, as illness, as a boil, as an arrow, as evil, as an affliction, as alien, as empty, as soulless. He turns his mind away from these things.'[3]

To the modern Buddhist, who may just have been mindfully savouring his breakfast, while carefully attending to his wounded inner child with mindful self-compassion, this teaching would come as a shock, as an anathema. Did the Buddha really say *that*? Where, to put it bluntly, is the love in this passage? Surely this cannot be Buddhism? And although there are many texts from the original Buddhist writings which are far

---

[2] See the excellent article by Ronald Purser, *The Myth of the Present Moment*, for the difference between a more traditional understanding of 'mindfulness' and the current over-emphasis on the present moment in mindfulness' most contemporary forms
(https://link.springer.com/article/10.1007/s12671-014-0333-z).
[3] *Majjhima Nikaya* I 435, in the book *Pali Buddhist Texts*, 37.

more life-affirming and compassionate, these words *were* part of the Buddha's teachings, part of his worldview in which the ultimate aim was to escape the cyclical nature of existence, or samsara. To the modern, Western Buddhist, who often proudly claims that Buddhism is not a religion, but rather a philosophy as a way of life, coming face to face with such texts can be disturbing.

But that the Western Buddhist's worldview can be so different - at least in certain ways - to that of the Buddha's is, however, not surprising when we consider that Buddhism itself is a highly malleable system, adapting itself, as it does, to whichever new culture it finds itself in. For, of all the world religions, Buddhism is arguably the most malleable and culturally specific. Across the Eastern cultures, strikingly different forms of Buddhism exist: Japanese Zen Buddhism is as different from Tibetan Buddhism as Tibetan Buddhism is from Theravadan Buddhism. As Storhoff, a scholar of Buddhism, explains: 'Historically, Buddhism has evolved wherever it has spread, responding as a vital and dynamic religion to local customs and emotional needs.'[4] That is not to say that there is not a common thread to all of these different manifestations of Buddhism but the key point is that they *are* noticeably different manifestations.

And so the question becomes: what are the specific needs that we, in the modern world have, and how have these needs led us to reshape Buddhism? What does a 'Western' Buddhism look like?

---

[4] Storhoff, 2013 (3).

The answer is an approach that is quite different to the Buddhism advocated by the Buddha (even if it is very much in his spirit). Let us take three key modern-day Buddhist authors, and consider what is distinctively different about their approach vis à vis traditional Buddhism. They are Stephen Batchelor, Jack Kornfield and Thich Nhat Hanh. I have chosen these three teachers as representative of 'Western Buddhism' not only because all three are very popular and much respected Buddhist teachers in the West but also because all three are deliberately and intentionally engaging in a process of 'reinventing' Buddhism for a Western audience. These three teachers, when taken together, are representative of the 'Western Buddhism' which I consider in this book. There are, of course, other representations of Buddhism in the West, including more Classical forms, but the kind of ideas found in these three authors are arguably indicative of its most popular forms in Western society.

Stephen Batchelor & The Argument for Secular Buddhism

In considering first Stephen Batchelor, we find a teacher who is emblematic of the kind of Modern Buddhist approach I am describing. Having spent a considerable portion of his early adult life as a Buddhist monastic (first in the Tibetan and then in the Korean Zen traditions), he disrobed and became a teacher and proponent of 'secular Buddhism'. Author of several controversial books, including *Confession of a Buddhist Atheist* and *Buddhism Without Beliefs*, he is most well-known for his radical confrontations with more traditional understandings of Buddhism. For Batchelor, Buddhism cannot afford to become rigid and ossify into overly traditionalist forms. Rather, the very core teaching of Buddhism, that of impermanence, must be applied not just to our understanding of life, but to the system of Buddhism itself: Buddhism too is impermanent, devoid of a fixed essence, requiring of change.[5] 'Because the Buddha said so' is not an adequate explanation for Batchelor. One might suggest that he is more interested in what 'the Buddha would have said', had he been alive today in our own culture. In that sense, Batchelor refers to himself as a 'secular' Buddhist. By this, he does not mean simply 'non-religious'. Rather, he means his Buddhism is informed by the needs and requirements 'of this age', the original meaning of the Latin word 'saeculum'.[6] To give one particularly striking example of how this informs Batchelor's teaching, his approach has led him to explicitly reject any conception of reincarnation, an orthodox tenet of traditional Buddhism. Rather, he argues that belief in rebirth is simply unnecessary. Defining Buddhism instead as primarily a 'practice' or means to manage and overcome suffering (or 'anguish'), he writes:

> 'It is odd that a practice concerned with anguish and the ending of anguish should be obliged to adopt ancient Indian metaphysical theories and thus accept as an article of faith that consciousness cannot be explained in terms of brain function.'[7]

---

[5] 2011b, 278.
[6] See Stephen Batchelor's piece here:
http://yalebooksblog.co.uk/2017/04/03/secular-buddhism-by-stephen-batchelor-an-extract/
[7] 1997, 37.

In this position, 'consciousness' does not pass from one animate being to another at death, but can instead be explained purely scientifically, in terms, as Batchelor puts it, of 'brain function'. And if the heart of Buddhism is indeed defined as the practical and therapeutic means by which 'anguish' (Batchelor's preferred translation of 'Dukkha', normally translated as 'suffering') can be understood and eased, then any such additional belief in reincarnation becomes surplus to requirements. Batchelor is hardly alone in this view. Most (although not all) Western Buddhists also reject the possibility of reincarnation: it simply does not chime with the scientific and rationalistic culture in which they have grown up.

So how can we characterise Batchelor's Buddhism? His concern is eminently practical: how do we respond to 'the existential condition of anguish'[8] we find ourselves in? In his readings of the Classical Buddhist texts, he has selected and reworked a wide range of texts which can fit within this more focussed framework, discarding many others which do not. One such original text which has inspired Batchelor's approach in this regard is the Buddha's comparison of the Dharma (the Buddhist word for 'truth' or 'teaching' - essentially the means by which suffering is understood and overcome) to a raft which you make yourself in order to get to the other side of the river.[9] Concerning this, Batchelor writes that a modern Buddhist practice entails collecting:

---

[8] 1997, 6.
[9] *Majjhima Nikaya* 22, i. 135.

> '...ideas, images, insights, philosophical styles, meditation methods and ethical values that you find here and there in Buddhism, bind(ing) them securely together, then launch(ing) your raft into the river of your life. As long as it does not sink or disintegrate and can get you to the other shore, then it works. It need not correspond to anyone else's idea of what 'Buddhism' is or should be.'[10]

It is easy to see why this open ended and flexible approach resonates with the modern-day preference for personal inquiry and, to a considerable degree also, Western individualism.

The overtly practical focus also resonates. For Bathcelor, the Buddha's Four Noble Truths are not beliefs to be accepted on blind faith, but rather 'Four Noble *Tasks*' to be worked out and actively applied.[11] Batchelor's argument is that the core aspects of Buddhism need to be reworked in light of our own cultural norms. The resulting 'Buddhism' is not, in Batchelor's view, antagonistic to the Buddhism of the Buddha. Rather, it takes the key insights into the nature of reality and the mind which the Buddha uncovered and adapts these to the modern day. It is simply an attempt to put forward a Buddhism for the 21st century which the Buddha himself, were he around today, would have approved of.

Batchelor's conscious reworking of Buddhism is epitomized by the following Zen koan, first used by a 12th century Zen monk called Yun Men, and quoted by Batchelor to support his arguments. Yun Men was

---

[10] 2011a, 229
[11] See: https://www.upaya.org/2015/02/stephen-batchelor-four-noble-tasks/

asked 'What are the teachings of a whole lifetime?' And in his concise yet profound response, '...an appropriate statement',[12] we can detect the basis for 'Western' Buddhism itself.

Jack Kornfield & Adapting Buddhism for Western Psychology

Jack Kornfield is our second 'Western Buddhist' teacher. Like Stephen Batchelor, he had extensive experience of Buddhist monasticism through his time as a student and monk of Ajahn Chah in Thailand, a leading monastic teacher in the Thai Forest tradition. However, Kornfield returned to America and, in 1976, founded the Insight Meditation tradition along with a small group of other Americans.[13] The process of adapting Buddhism for the Western mind has been a key aspect of his approach and one of his most well-known books, and one which I draw upon in this reflection, is entitled *A Path with Heart: Buddhist Psychology for the West*.

As with Batchelor, Kornfield struggled with the rigid and monastic forms of Buddhism he was a part of in his early adult life. Calling out in particular the difficulties he had with the predominant approaches of Buddhist hierarchies in Asia, he later wrote of his experience as follows:

> 'What I have struggled with are the limitations of Buddhism as an organized religion; with the sectarianism and attachments of many of the students and teachers involved; and with the

---

[12] 1997, 45.
[13] Batchelor (2011b), 349.

territoriality, the patriarchy, and the excessive life-denying tendencies of practice that can leave it, and some students, disconnected from their hearts.'[14]

In these words, we can detect Kornfield's struggle both to find a form of Buddhism which was able to connect *in a heartfelt way* with the engaged realities of daily life for someone living outside of a monastic context and to find a philosophical system which encouraged individual enquiry. Indeed, Kornfield considers that it is essential to reconsider and rework those areas of traditional Buddhism which are - as he puts it strongly - 'weak or medieval'.[15]

These kinds of concerns were motivating factors in the setting up of the Insight Meditation community in America. He describes the process of adapting Buddhism to the North American mind as follows:

'...we've learned and attempted to bring the clearest and most straightforward version of Buddhist practice to the West. We left much of the ritual, Eastern culture, and ceremony behind in Asia. This is not because we don't value it...but we felt it was unnecessary. It seemed to us that for our time and culture the simplicity and straightforwardness of mindfulness practice itself would speak best to the heart of North Americans.'[16]

Undoubtedly, Kornfield was correct to focus on the 'simplicity and straightforwardness' of mindfulness practice as speaking to his 'time and culture'. Indeed, many who come to Buddhism in the West are attracted to it precisely because (for the most part) there is little

---

[14] 2011, 199-200.
[15] 2011, 201.
[16] In Stevenson (1991), 248.

or no ceremony or ritual on display. Furthermore, many spiritual seekers today do not wish to be 'told all the answers' through a doctrine of 'revealed religious truth' but rather to make use of practices and insights to both transform their inner selves and encourage more heartfelt relationships with others. It is probably for this reason that Western Buddhism tends to highlight, first and foremost, the practice of mindfulness. Indeed, it is notable that mindfulness is the cornerstone and pillar of so many Buddhist groups in the West, whereas the other seven pillars of the Buddha's Noble Eight-fold Path tend (although not always) to be less emphasized. For the Buddha, Right View, Right Intention, Right Speech, Right Action, Right Livelihood, Right Effort, Right Mindfulness and Right Concentration were all equally important aspects of his teachings and you could not have one without the others. However, the Western appropriation of Buddhist teachings has tended to focus first and foremost on the practice of meditation and on the cultivation of mindfulness in daily life. In contrast, in traditional Buddhist cultures, lay Buddhists most often do not practice meditation, leaving that to the monks, and focus instead on living with the principles of right livelihood and following ethical precepts in their day-to-day lives.

For Kornfield, stripping Buddhism of its dogmatic and overly traditionalist features is an act of '...courage on the part of North American Buddhists.'[17] But it has not just entailed removing those aspects of Buddhism

---

[17] 2011, 201.

that may seem to be objectionable in a Western context but also inserting new progressive Western ideals into the fabric of Buddhism itself. For Kornfield, this includes encouraging the idea of shared Buddhist practice (i.e. non-sectarianism between different forms of Buddhism), democritization, feminization and integration (into daily life and social action in society at large).[18] All of these ideals, including those inspired by Western ideals of equality, have become part of what it means to be a Western Buddhist and inform its practice of extending compassion towards others. It is perhaps ironic that many Western Buddhists may not realize that many of the ethical ideals in their philosophy in fact owe a considerable amount not just to the Buddha himself but also to the progressive ideals that have their basis in Western society.

Thich Nhat Hanh: Developing an Engaged Buddhism

Thich Nhat Hanh is a Vietnamese monk who, along with the Dalai Lama, is arguably one of the most famous Buddhist teachers alive today and one of the leading proponents of 'Engaged Buddhism'. By this I mean not only a form of Buddhism that actively applies itself to the very real, tangible suffering and problems of daily life but also a form of Buddhism which engages with social injustices, humanitarian crises and the destructions of war.[19] Having trained as a monk in a more traditional monastic setting, this represents Thich Nhat Hanh's attempt to 'think outside the

---
[18] 2011, 195ff.
[19] King, 2011, 74.

monastic box', creating an approach which anyone, potentially, could adopt as their way of life. He was like this from the beginning. As a young monk in Vietnam, he continually challenged the status quo, calling on Buddhist hierarchies to include Western philosophy and science in the monastic curriculum, arguing that these subjects would help 'infuse life into the practice of Buddhism.'[20] Ultimately, he founded his own community, which later became known as the 'Order of Interbeing', a form of Buddhism which Thich Nhat Hanh explicitly hopes '...may be accepted...in the West.'[21] Within the Order of Interbeing, there exist several living communities which Thich Nhat Hanh considers to be models for 'social change',[22] the most notable of which is Plum Village in France. To join the 'Order of Interbeing', the practitioner can subscribe to the *Five Mindfulness Trainings*, 'a Buddhist vision for a global spirituality and ethic,'[23] or, if they wish to deepen their practice, to the *Fourteen Mindfulness Trainings*.

Thich Nhat Hanh's version of Buddhism takes many of the traditional Buddhist teachings and reworks them with a 'positive spin'. For example, he has playfully (yet seriously) reworked the Buddha's First Noble Truth, 'Life is Suffering', when he writes: 'To suffer is not enough. We must also be in touch with the wonders of life.'[24] Likewise, he regards impermanence as a key factor in promoting *positive* change:

---

[20] King, 2001, 73.
[21] 1995, 86.
[22] King, 2001, 82.
[23] See: https://plumvillage.org/mindfulness-practice/the-5-mindfulness-trainings/
[24] 1995, 13.

'Long live impermanence! Without it, nothing is possible!'[25] Similarly, like Batchelor, he does not focus on rebirth. Again, preferring a practical approach, he writes: 'We do not practice for the sake of the future, to be reborn...but to be peace, to be compassion, to be joy right now.'[26] In Western Buddhism, the originally orthodox belief in rebirth has become unorthodox, the exception rather than the norm.

Thich Nhat Hanh's approach is very explicitly aimed at appealing to the requirements of the Western spiritual seeker. Since adaptation is an essential part of Buddhism's very nature, Thich Nhat Hanh believes that each form of Buddhism should correlate to the culture in which it finds itself. 'The forms of Buddhism,' he writes, 'must change so that the essence of Buddhism remains unchanged. This essence consists of living principles that cannot bear any specific formulation.'[27] Indeed, while visiting America, he made a point of enquiring about when a statue of an 'American Buddha' would ever appear.[28] Furthermore, to his American readership, he writes: 'I think we can learn from other Buddhist traditions, but you have to create your own Buddhism. I believe that out of deep practice you will have your own Buddhism very soon.'[29] In short, Thich Nhat Hanh is a proponent of a form of Buddhism strikingly different from that of his own monastic background: it is engaged, societal and adapted to underlying Western beliefs and spiritual needs.

---

[25] In an interview on the *Dharma Gates* website (http://dharmagates.org/long_live_impermanence.html).
[26] 1995, 88.
[27] In Batchelor (2011b), 274.
[28] 1995, 85.
[29] 1995, 86.

Towards an Understanding of 'Western' Buddhism

With the consideration of these three teachers in place, how can we best understand 'Western' Buddhism?

Perhaps the most striking aspect of Western Buddhism which is evident in all three of our teachers is its highly *selective* approach. Only those ideas and concepts in the original Buddhist texts *which resonate* (i.e. those texts which serve in some sense the spiritual dilemmas of the West today) are included in the Western Buddhist literature. Plenty is left behind: many of the traditional rites and rituals, hierarchical systems, metaphysical worldviews - even many key traditional Buddhist ethical ideas are downplayed (you *may* hear a Western Buddhist talk about the importance of cultivating 'Right Livelihood' but he is far more *likely* to talk of mindfulness). Instead, we have a philosophy which encourages self-transformation through meditative practices (along with the cultivation of compassion) and a spirit of largely personal enquiry.

On this last point, the spirit of personal enquiry, let us consider a very instructive example of Western Buddhism's highly selective approach with its source texts. Often, in attending a Buddhist group in the West, you will hear that the Buddha emphasized the importance of personal enquiry and finding out for yourself whether his teachings were true or not. This stems in part from an extract from the *Majjhima Nikaya (The Collection of Middle-Length Discourses)*, in which the Buddha emphasizes the importance of trusting one's own experience rather than blindly following what your teacher tells you:

> "'Monks, would you perhaps, when you know and see this, speak so: 'Our teacher is venerable and we speak out of respect for our teacher?"
> "Certainly not, sir!"
> (...)
> "Monks do you not speak that which is known by yourselves, seen by yourselves, found by yourselves!"
> "Yes, sir!"'[30]

The *Kalama Sutta* (*Teaching to the Kalamas*) encourages likewise: never accept something because your teacher says so, but only when you know it for yourself.[31] Although these passages are undoubtedly true to the spirit of the Buddha's teachings, it is ironic that these passages are popular in Western and not, by and large, in traditional Buddhism. As the scholar of contemporary Buddhism McMahan notes in his book *The Making of Buddhist Modernism*, the old texts that emphasized personal enquiry never enjoyed popularity '...prior to the modern age,'[32] and Buddhists historically '...have not been encouraged to question orthodox doctrine or to construct their own personal approach to the path.'[33] Rather, certain ideas from the ancient sources have been 'cherry-picked' and reworked into a form of Buddhist practice which emphasizes personal enquiry.

---

[30] *Majjhima Nikaya* I 265 in the book *Pali Buddhist Texts*, 19-20.
[31] *Kalama Sutta*, in Batchelor (1997), 1.
[32] 2008, 65.
[33] 2008, 44.

McMahan's ideas will further help us. In short, he argues that 'Buddhist Modernism' is the result, by and large, of the following three factors: *detraditionalization*, *demythologization* and *psychologization*. Of the first, he writes that, after the Romantic and Rationalist movements, the western mind finds it difficult to accept a 'transcendent and authoritative past'. Instead, Buddhism is 'detraditionalised' such that '...the "self" itself...is considered sacred, and the internal realm becomes the locus of authority.' Likewise, a system that is 'demythologized' reads myth as metaphor for different states of mind rather than fact, and in one that is 'psychologized', the emphasis is placed on cultivating psychological health. The contrast is perhaps most explicit when one considers that centuries ago Western academia (in a rather prejudiced and typically general way) first characterized Buddhism as '...atheistic, nihilistic, quietistic, pessimistic and idolatrous', while today most Buddhist practitioners in the West would see their philosophy as '...optimistic, activist, anti-ritualistic, anti-idolatry, and socially beneficial.'[34]

One clear indication that Western Buddhism is an adaptation is that very few original Buddhist texts are studied in detail in Western Buddhist groups (for the most part). Rather, certain key stories, extracts and parables from the Buddha tend to be discussed along with a standard set of instructions on meditation and mindfulness practice. Furthermore, most books by modern day Western Buddhists do not draw extensively on the original Buddhist texts. Rather, they draw on

---

[34] 2008: 43 ('transcendent and authoritative past', 43 'locus of authority', 46- metaphor, 40 [psychological health], 69 [contrast in perception of Buddhism by early Western academia and modern-day practitioners].

some original, key Buddhist ideas, the author's own experience and personal philosophy as well as insights from other spiritual traditions and Western psychotherapy. This is a clear indication that Western Buddhism is an 'adaptation' as so little attention, relatively speaking, is spent considering the old, original texts. Indeed, it is rare that you might meet a Western Buddhist who has carefully studied the *Pali Canon*. He is more likely to be a follower of, say, Thich Nhat Hanh or Jack Kornfield, or to have developed an approach which draws on many different contemporary Buddhist teachers from here and there. This is very much in line with the non-dogmatic nature of Western Buddhism and its emphasis on personal enquiry.

In discussing the nature of Buddhism in the West, I wish to make clear that I am not in any way implying that 'Western Buddhism' is 'superior' to other variations of Buddhism found throughout the world both now and historically. Rather, I am simply trying to describe the salient features of a form of Buddhism which has come 'out of the wash' following a meeting of Western culture with the Buddha's teachings. It is as it is, and nor is confined geographically to the West. In an age of globalization and the mass sharing of ideas over the internet, the kind of Buddhism under discussion is becoming prevalent in all corners of the globe. Furthermore, it is important to emphasise, as I have already done, that 'Western Buddhism' is by no means anathema to the Buddha's own philosophy. The approach of Western Buddhism is very much in the spirit of the Buddha's own teachings, but these have just been adapted to have a specific Western 'hue'.

In summary, in Western Buddhism we have a wholly practical approach aimed at coping with suffering as it arises in daily life and as an existential reality. High level personal enquiry is not confined to a select few within the monastic walls but is accessible to all. The transformative practice of mindfulness is brought to the fore, whereas traditionally it tended to be reserved for monks. Similarly, in traditional Buddhism, lay Buddhist practitioners tend to focus on accumulating 'merit' through good deeds so as to (ideally) have a positive future rebirth, whereas in Western Buddhism the focus is instead on a 'here and now' philosophy where belief in reincarnation is not essential and is, in fact, rare. Indeed, Western Buddhism is very much associated with encouraging a focus on the present moment ('the only moment you ever have is now' is one expression of this idea) although this aspect of mindfulness was not stressed by the Buddha himself. Western Buddhism is, in short, a wholly practical philosophy as a way of life, complete with meditative exercises to encourage transformation of the self, along with ethical principles which also encourage instilling positive change in society at large.

And if all that reminds you of the aims of Stoicism, then you wouldn't be too far wrong.

Stoicism & Its Modern-Day 'Reinvention'

Stoicism is, and always was, a highly practical philosophy as a way of life. Its key idea is that the most important thing we should value in life is virtue, or, put more straightforwardly, maintaining an excellent state of character and wise action in the face of whatever life throws at us. Along with this, it has many techniques and exercises to encourage transformation of the self in ways analogous, albeit not the same, to Buddhist meditation practices.

The texts of Marcus Aurelius' *Meditations*, the private Stoic reflections of the Roman emperor to himself, the *Discourses* of Epictetus, the freed-slave turned philosopher, and the *Letters* of Seneca, the Statesman, have always been popular, but today they are finding renewed life. This is, in large part, thanks to the *Modern Stoicism* movement (also known as *Stoicism Today*), a group of psychotherapists, academics and philosophers, who, since 2012, have been developing modern-day Stoic resources and activities, including an International Stoic Week held once a year (currently in October). Stoic Week regularly attracts thousands of participants worldwide who follow a specially designed *Handbook* of modernized Stoic advice.[35]

But is this new form of Stoicism the same as the Stoicism of Marcus Aurelius, Epictetus or Seneca? Or has there been, in ways perhaps similar to the case of Western Buddhism, a 'reinvention' of Stoicism such that it is adapting itself to the specific spiritual dilemmas of the modern West?

The answer to that is 'yes'. As Western Buddhism has dropped aspects of traditional Buddhist practice and beliefs, such as reincarnation, in favour of more applied and practical ideas, so too has Modern Stoicism dropped significant aspects of the ancient version of the philosophy. And, in particular, there has been one very significant change.

---

[35] For more about Stoic Week and the Modern Stoicism movement, see: www.modernstoicism.com.

Taking God Out of Stoicism

From the perspective of many who practise Stoicism today, the main 'problem' with the Ancient Stoic is that he believed in a divine principle which permeated all living things. This divine principle, the 'Logos', was called various titles by the Stoics: 'Zeus', 'God', 'Nature'. It is best understood as a principle, an ordered 'life force' which runs through all things. Unlike the Judaeo-Christian God, you could not enter into a 'personal relationship' with the Stoic Logos, and you certainly could not ask it 'for any favours': the Stoic divine principle was wholly impersonal. But, as an Ancient Stoic, you would definitely have been in awe of the Logos' divinely structured workings, the amazing coherence found within Nature, and the logical ways in which the world seemed to have been put together. The Stoic, in this sense, undoubtedly did worship the Logos.

Not only this, however, but the ancient Stoic also considered himself to be a living manifestation of the Logos and this consideration led him to cultivate his own inner divinity, as a 'living spark' of the divine. The divine spark within each of us was considered to be a kind of innate 'inner goodness'. Epictetus put it this way: 'Whenever you close your doors and make darkness within, remember never to say that you are alone. For you are not alone, indeed God is within you and is your inner guardian.'[36] The idea of an 'inner divinity' runs throughout Stoicism, and its writings are full of references to God and Nature understood as a providential force.

---

[36] Epictetus, *Discourses*, 1.14.2.

For many today, these kinds of ideas will chime well with theistic beliefs already held. For many others, however, ancient Stoicism's belief in God will be a stumbling block that is deeply problematic in ways similar to the difficulties many Western Buddhists have with the concept of reincarnation. And so anyone who is inspired by the ancient Stoic texts, but not by their theistic underpinnings, is left with a choice: do I turn my back on Stoicism completely or do I try to use some parts of the philosophy while leaving others? And if the latter course is taken, is a form of Stoicism without 'God' still 'Stoicism' or does the philosophy become something else entirely?

The Arguments For & Against Taking God out of Stoicism

An interesting exchange occurred on this exact question between Mark Vernon, author of books on philosophy and psychotherapy, and Tim LeBon, a psychotherapist and member of the *Modern Stoicism* team. These two articles were originally framed as a kind of 'debate' between the authors on the *Stoicism Today* blog in November 2014 and are indicative of the kind of arguments you might hear on both sides of this question.

In his article entitled 'In Praise of the Logos', Vernon is critical of Modern Stoicism's removal of God from the philosophy, writing that this removal is deeply antagonistic to its roots:

> '...ancient Stoics did not believe that it is possible to live contentedly largely by ignoring what you can't control, as Stoicism is sometimes interpreted

today. They did not presume that those most human of feelings - fear and anger - are simply our personal choices, to be turned off and on by some trained trick of the will. They saw that life can gradually be re-ordered to serve a deeper, divine imperative that runs through all things. Let go into that fundamental goodness, and whatever happens will ultimately be shaped after its beneficent, magnificent pattern. It's a commitment of faith to a changed perception of life, not a commitment to reprogramming aimed at a personality adjustment, again as Stoicism can sometimes seem to its modern advocates.'[37]

In the same article, Vernon adds further that:

'To be frank, I think it is disingenuous if not dishonest to sideline the divine foundations. It turns Stoicism into an atmosphere without air, a sea without water. Such reductionism is doubly misleading when it comes to Stoicism because the Stoics prided themselves on their rational approach to life that adds up because all its different parts link together - physics, ethics and metaphysics. Drop one element and they felt you are on the way to losing the lot.'[38]

Seen like this, the very strength of Stoicism is that it is a theistic philosophy and that, as such, it is challenging us to see *its* deeply thought out metaphysical point of view. God was not an 'optional extra' in ancient Stoicism and nor should it be in any modern form of Stoicism. Rather, belief in God was at the heart of the entire philosophy and this belief encouraged Stoicism's adherents to reorder their life entirely, centering it around the Logos. Furthermore, for Vernon, the belief in God and the Stoic conception of ethics were inter-

---

[37] In Ussher, 2016, 215.
[38] In Ussher, 2016, 218.

related: living with virtue depends on understanding one's place in a cosmos that was created, and remains permeated, by God. And so, in creating a Stoicism without God, are we left with an 'atmosphere without air' or a 'sea without water'? In other words, is a form of Stoicism without God really 'Stoicism' at all?

For LeBon, this question misses the point. Rather, the most important point is the fact that, unlike in Ancient Greece or Rome, we now do live in a society in which many no longer believe in God. Given this fact, these 'changed circumstances', is it not incumbent upon us to find a way to still make Stoicism work for the many atheists or agnostics who may turn to it for advice? In his opening response to Vernon's piece, he writes:

> 'How many twenty-first century readers can accept the claims made in the following ancient Stoic passage quoted approvingly by Mark Vernon in the previous piece?
>
>> "The whole universe, spinning around the earth, goes wherever you [Zeus] lead it and is willingly guided by you."
>
> How many of us can believe that the universe spins round the earth? How many of us believe that Zeus is in charge of our fate?
>
> I imagine that very few modern-day readers will accept these and some of the other metaphysical claims made by the ancient Stoics. Logic therefore dictates that we have a choice. We could discard Stoicism on the grounds that it is based on claims that we can no longer believe. The title of this article - "In Praise of Modern Stoicism" - suggests an alternative. Rather than abandon Stoicism we can and should develop a modern, acceptable and helpful form of Stoicism.'[39]

---

[39] In Ussher, 2016, 221.

This is a question of practicality. The cultural norm for the Ancient Greeks was to believe in the Divine, in many different forms, but that is not our cultural norm, which is instead far more pluralistic and, for many, atheistic. Given this, should Stoicism only be accessible to those who believe in God?

For LeBon and for the Modern Stoicism project, the main Stoic idea that virtue is the most important thing in life can stand alone, irrespective of any belief in God. In other words, the idea that there is a wise and skilful way to respond to events, no matter what the circumstances, is an idea that does not require a belief in God, even if, in ancient Stoicism, living virtuously did also imply accepting, in some ways, that belief. The *Stoic Week Handbook* explains the importance of virtue as follows:

> 'The central Stoic claim was that virtue is ultimately the only thing that really matters; it is the only thing that is truly good, and it is the only thing that can bring us well-being and fulfillment. Cultivating virtue ought to be our top priority, above all other things, if we want to live a good life. The Stoics used the word *eudaimonia* to describe someone who lives the best type of life. It's usually translated as "happiness". However, it doesn't refer to a happy feeling but rather something more rounded and complete. Some people think that "flourishing" or "fulfillment" are better translations. You can also think of *eudaimonia* as meaning "happiness" in the archaic sense, the opposite of being in a "hapless" or wretched condition.'[40]

This is not, therefore, just about 'personality adjustment' but about changing your deepest values to prioritize,

---

[40] *Stoic Week 2017 Handbook*, p. 10.

above all, having an excellent state of character in the face of events. And, in the Modern Stoicism movement, only those ancient Stoic texts which explicitly focus on virtue, character change, values and transformation of the self tend to be focussed on.

Furthermore, LeBon also argues that we should study what are the most helpful aspects of Stoicism, the most useful 'active ingredients' of the philosophy. From his research with Stoic Week participants, LeBon concludes that those are: 'Stoic mindfulness (making an effort to pay continual attention to the nature of my judgements and actions)', 'Stoic disputation of thoughts (reminding oneself that an upsetting thought is just an impression in my mind and not the thing it claims to represent'), 'Affinity with others (thinking of oneself as part of the human race, in the same way that a limb is a part of the human body)', 'Stoic Premeditation (trying to anticipate future misfortunes and rehearse rising above them).'[41] These elements are all eminently practical and none of them require acceptance of ancient metaphysical beliefs. In the same way that it is unnecessary to believe in reincarnation to find a form of Buddhism which deals with the 'existential condition of anguish' (to borrow Batchelor's terminology) so too is it, in LeBon's view, unnecessary to regard as credible the Stoic conception of a divine principle which permeates all things in order to use Stoic techniques, ideas, and ethics to meet life's challenges better. However, this 'reinvention' of Stoicism does not preclude someone from following every aspect of

---

[41] In Ussher, 2016, 222.

traditional Stoicism, should they so wish. As LeBon writes: 'You can be religious and follow Modern Stoicism, but you don't have to be.'[42] This is a 'broad tent' conception of Stoicism.

Conclusion: Two Similar Adaptations, Two Similar Philosophies

As we have seen, the reshaping of both philosophies following their respective meetings with modern, Western culture, has contained remarkably similar processes. In both cases, certain aspects of the ancient philosophies have been regarded as no longer relevant, as 'ossified baggage', and, in both cases, these elements have been dropped. Rather than being key to what life is all about, the Stoic God and Buddhist Reincarnation are now to be 'added in' according to personal preference. Instead, those aspects of both philosophies which are most applicable to daily life and to inner transformation have been emphasized.

The result is two highly practical philosophies as a way of life which, although they of course contain important differences, are noticeably similar to each other in many ways. Indeed, while it might be harder for a comparison of ancient Stoicism and ancient Buddhism to find as much common ground between the two philosophies, the 'reinventions' of both philosophies following their meeting with modern, Western culture, are much more similar to each other. In the next three chapters, I will mainly focus on presenting these similarities between both approaches in a way that I hope will be of interest and help.

---

[42] In Ussher, 2016, 225.

On the Stoic side, I will be focusing mainly on original texts: those of Seneca and particularly Epictetus and Marcus Aurelius. I will be discussing writings from these authors which would resonate with the Modern Stoicism movement, i.e. the texts I have chosen to discuss do not contain a focus on God. Rather, the writings chosen remain focussed on ethics. Furthermore, these are the three authors who have most influenced the Modern Stoicism movement I described above and whose approach implicitly and explicitly informs the Stoic Week Handbook and other modern-day Stoic books such as *Stoicism & The Art of Happiness* by Donald Robertson, *How to be a Stoic* by Massimo Pigluicci and *The Obstacle is the Way* by Ryan Holiday.

On the Buddhist side, I will make use of extracts from the Buddha which are commonly used in Western Buddhism, although I shall mainly focus on select works of Thich Nhat Hanh, Jack Kornfield and Stephen Batchelor, our trio of Buddhist teachers discussed above, all of whom are knowingly engaged in an ongoing adaptation of Buddhism for a Western audience.

More specifically, in chapter one, 'A Similar Spirit', I will consider what psychological foundations both systems share and to what extent the two philosophies operate in a shared spirit. I will consider how both philosophies hold that life is, put simply, hard but that there are ways to cultivate a flourishing life nevertheless and to make ethical progress in life, and that this largely depends on developing greater self-awareness, paying attention to the workings of our mind, and staying open to opportunities for self-transformation.

In chapter two, 'Mindfulness in Stoicism & Buddhism', I will consider how the Stoic and Buddhist respectively approaches self-change and what kind of ethical development each is aiming at. I will also explore the different philosophical exercises and meditative techniques which are used in each system and how they might mutually inform each other. What, for example, is the difference between Stoic and Buddhist 'mindfulness'?

In chapter three, 'Cultivating Compassion', I will consider how each philosophy understands the place of the self in relation to others and how, paradoxically, concern for others is instrumental in self-development and, furthermore, I will discuss the techniques, tools and insights by which each system encourages the development of concern and compassion for others. In many ways, in this chapter we will explore the heart of both Stoicism and Western Buddhism.

Finally, I will conclude this essay with further reflections on the nature of the ongoing adaptations of Stoicism and Buddhism in the modern world as well as in what ways I believe both systems have ideas, tools and insights that can be mutually informative.

Chapter One

A Similar Spirit

'Conditioned things break down, tread the path with care.'[43]

The Buddha

'Do not act as if you had ten thousand years to live...while you still have life in you, while you still can, make yourself good.'[44]

Marcus Aurelius

Both Stoicism and Buddhism are therapeutic philosophies. Epictetus' 'healing place for sick souls' is akin to Buddhism's own perceived function of itself as 'medical diagnosis, prognosis and treatment,'[45] where the Buddha is seen as a 'physician'.[46] The student comes with his problems - from his daily life, his existential state, his relationships - to his teacher in order to be 'treated'.

The advice given will not necessarily be easy to take though, let alone to implement. For, as can be gathered from both quotations above, there are no platitudes to be found in either 'therapy'. Batchelor considers

---

[43] *Digha Nikaya* (*Collection of Long Discourses*), 16. ii 156.
[44] *Meditations*, 4.17.
[45] Batchelor (1997), 6.
[46] Thich Nhat Hanh (1998), 44.

Buddhism to lead more to *confrontation* (with the realities of existence) than to *consolation* (from belief-sets).[47] In other words, Buddhism takes on the hard realities of suffering, ill-health and death and tries to find a way to live well within those realities, rather than offering hope in, for example, an afterlife where none of these hardships exist. He cites a widely practised Buddhist reflection in this regard: 'Since death alone is certain, and the time of death is uncertain, what should I do?'[48] Similarly, Stoicism considers it essential to start from *the way things are*, equipping the practitioner to work with reality rather than against it. As Marcus Aurelius writes: 'How ridiculous and ignorant of the world is one who is surprised at anything that comes to pass in life.'[49] We need to recognise that life is not meant to be an easy journey, and that, nevertheless, somehow we need to find a way to live a good and flourishing life despite its inherent difficulties.

We need to understand life in its totality: what *all* of it is about. In this regard, Batchelor cites the Buddha's parable of *The Elephant*,[50] which compares typical efforts to understand dharma ('truth' or 'reality') with three blind men who attempt to describe an elephant using only their sense of touch. One is presented with an ear to feel, another a tusk, another the trunk, and so on. The central part of the parable runs as follows:

---

[47] 1997, 18.
[48] 1997, 29.
[49] *Meditations*, 12.13. Cf. 10.28.
[50] *Udana* (*Inspired Utterances*), 6.4.

> 'Then the king approached the blind people and said: "Tell me, blind people, what is an elephant like?"
>
> Those blind people who had been shown the head of the elephant replied: "An elephant is just like a water jar..." "just like a winnowing basket..." "just like a ploughshare..." [and so on].
>
> 'Saying "An elephant is like this, an elephant is not like that!" "An elephant is not like this, an elephant is like that!" they fought each other with their fists!
>
> And the king was delighted (with this spectacle).'

One of the main points of this parable is that reality cannot be 'fragmented' into theories which limit engagement with life. For that approach encourages arguments over which philosophical 'view' of life is better or worse, an approach which induces a kind of philosophical 'blindness'. The Buddha's message in this instance is to drop such dogmatic tendencies that prevent us from seeing things *as they are in their totality*. Similarly, Marcus Aurelius, although operating within a wholly different cultural context, was also wary of any tendency to 'fragment' life. 'A healthy eye,' he writes, 'should look at all that can be seen and not say "I want green things alone", for that is the mark of a diseased eye....accordingly, a healthy mind should be ready for all that comes about.'[51] Both philosophies are upfront about the fact that we can't hide from life and what it brings. In philosophy as a way of life, *no* aspect of life can be ignored: we must accept the reality of what comes our way and try to find out how best to respond to this reality.

---

[51] *Meditations*, 10.35.

And, as I have just mentioned, this reality is not easy. Indeed, according to the Buddha's *First Noble Truth*, it is *Dukkha*,[52] a word which has been traditionally translated as 'Suffering' (although this translation has been challenged and qualified in modern Western Buddhism, as in the case of Stephen Batchelor who, as we have seen above, uses the term 'anguish'). However, in Pali it literally means a 'bad wheel' ('Du' - 'Bad' and 'Kha' - 'Wheel') and Buddhism is therefore concerned with the ending of a feeling that life is stuck, or not moving forward well. The Buddhist practitioner attempts to mitigate the effects of Dukkha through the practice of mindfulness, meditation and ethical precepts. In Stoicism, likewise, the path of Virtue is seen as resulting in the cessation of, it would not be a stretch to say, 'Dukkha'. For Epictetus' answer to 'What is the task of Virtue?' is the Greek word 'Eurhoia'[53] which literally means *a state of good flow*. This is essentially describing a life which is, therefore, not 'stuck'. Interestingly, in the ancient Buddhist writings, the opposite of 'Dukkha' is 'Sukha' which literally means a 'good wheel', implying a life which moves forward freely and which is unimpeded. In this sense, the life of 'Eurhoia' or the life of 'Sukha' are arguably seeking something similar. It is often how we respond to life that can lead us to feeling 'stuck' or 'trapped', in the same way that a faulty wheel might get stuck in the mud. Stoicism and Buddhism, in contrast, try to suggest ways that life can move towards becoming a continuous flow of unimpeded activity

---

[52] *Digha Nikaya* (*Collection of the Long Discourses*) II 305, from *Pali Buddhist Texts*, 23.
[53] *Discourses*, 1.4.6.

which wisely bends this way or that depending on the external circumstances we find ourselves in. And both claim that this possible, despite the fact that life is hard.

All this is the ideal. However, although we are all capable of such wise action, we are also all at a natural disadvantage. By this I mean that not only do both systems agree that life is difficult but they also agree that humans make it even *more* difficult for themselves by *craving* for life to be other than how it actually is. In Buddhism, the Second Noble Truth is that the origin of *Dukkha* is 'self-centered craving.'[54] Likewise, in Stoicism, craving for life to be other than how it is is the origin of emotional disturbance. In this light, Epictetus says: 'For this is the origin of suffering: to crave something and for it not to come about'.[55] Epictetus considers that the unhelpful mental states that result from such craving must be removed from life altogether. As he puts it, the task of the philosopher is as follows:

> '...to strive to remove from one's own life grief and lamentation, that shout of 'Oh poor me!' and 'oh how miserable I am!', and misfortune and failure.'[56]

For Epictetus, as for the Buddha, the philosophical path is about removing this kind of craving, which is really the result of a continuous self-preoccupation to have the universe accord with one's *own* wishes. Rather, we need to see what the universe brings us and then work out how best we can live within this reality.

---

[54] Batchelor (1997), 8.
[55] *Discourses*, 1.27.10
[56] *Discourses*, 1.4.23

In both philosophies, learning to live well or skilfully is paramount and involves careful practice of mental training, discipline and ethics. In Stoicism, this process happens little bit by little and is intimately connected with developing virtue. It is helpful to point out here that by 'virtue', the Stoics did not mean 'virtue' in the sense that we often think of it today, i.e. as an application of moral precepts (perhaps in a religious context). Rather, the ancient Greek word in question, 'arete', implies instead a kind of 'skill' or 'excellence' in the art of living. Stoic 'virtue' is about wise choices and maintaining an excellent state of mind and character in the face of life. And the application of this kind of 'virtue', although no easy task, is precisely what allows for life to 'flow well'. Similarly, in Western Buddhism, the following of 'ethical precepts' does not imply a rigid following of moral or religious rules. Rather, there is a clear rejection of the idea of 'absolute right or wrong' and instead the practice of mindfulness, in particular, encourages a focus on self-acceptance while also committing to working with one's own mind states in the most skilful way possible. 'Skilfulness' is a word often used in Western Buddhist gatherings and it refers to the ability to make the wisest possible use of one's thoughts and feelings and to craft the wisest course of action in any given circumstance.

In both philosophies, our progress along the path ebbs and flows although, ultimately, it can only happen *now*. When else? In Western Buddhism, awakening, although traditionally considered '...a long-term project',[57] is a state of being that permeates every-day life at certain moments. As Batchelor writes: 'Awakening is indeed close by - *and* supreme effort is required to realize it. Awakening is indeed far away - *and* readily accessible.'[58] Similarly, in Stoicism, the life of virtue is simultaneously both far away and close at hand. It easily returns when you can see a new and skilful way of responding to the current situation and act on that while it just as easily disappears when you find yourself 'stuck', when life is no longer 'flowing well'. In these ways, moments of awakening and of virtue arise and mark our lives in between periods of their absence.

Life Is As You Think It

In order to make ethical progress in life and 'skill at living well', we need first to turn our attention inwards: our outer life will be a reflection of our inner life. We need to understand how our minds work and how to cultivate our minds in deliberately skilful directions. Consider first Marcus Aurelius and then the often referenced opening lines of the *Dhammapada*, the earliest extant collection of sayings attributed to the Buddha. They run as follows:

> 'The character of your mind will be such as is the character of your frequent thoughts, for the soul takes its dye from thoughts.'[59]

---

[57] McMahan (2008), 40.
[58] 1997, 13.
[59] *Meditations*, 5.16.

'All that we are is the result of what we have thought: it is founded on our thoughts, it is made up of our thoughts.'[60]

From this, we can see two core aspects of psychology on which both Stoicism and Buddhism agree. Firstly, that one's concern should be with one's own mind for it determines how we see the world: everything [perception, thought, action] stems from within. And secondly, that one regards the mind as malleable - it can respond to our intentional choices and decisions and be deliberately 'cultivated' in wiser directions.

The first core aspect could also be summarised as *everything is mind.* By this I do not imply some kind of solipsism but rather a recognition of the basic fact that, as the scholar of Stoicism Anthony Long puts it, '...we do not experience the world without the mediation of our own assessments.'[61] This is a recurrent theme in Stoic thought, as a brief look at Marcus Aurelius demonstrates. His most famous maxim, 'The World is Change, *Life is Opinion*',[62] is one example. By this he means that the universe operates on the principle of impermanence, but each person's life is *as they think it*, and the quality of our lives depends on our values and conceptions. Take another example in which Marcus asks himself the following question: 'How is your ruling centre employing itself? For everything rests on that.'[63] [By the 'ruling centre', or 'hegemonikon' in Greek, the Stoics were referring to that part of the mind which can both witness our emotions and thoughts from a slight

---

[60] *Dhammapada*, 1.
[61] 2002, 28.
[62] *Discourses*, 3.4.4.
[63] *Discourses*, 12.33.

distance and deliberately choose to turn the mind in a new direction (modern science might call this 'Executive Function').] From this example, we see that our ability to take a step back and rethink things, to change our *conception* about things, is absolutely central to living a good life. For, as Marcus writes elsewhere, *hoti panta hupolepsis - everything is conception*. As we see the world so too is the world.

This is a common Buddhist idea and we find a helpful example of it in Stephen Batchelor also. He cites the Tibetan story of an old man at a loss as to how to practise the dharma. He has tried everything, including reading the scriptures and meditation, but has made no real progress. Disheartened, he approaches his teacher, Drom:

> 'With nothing else left to do, the old man asked:
>
> "Geshe-la, please, how should I practise the dharma?"
>
> "When you practice," Drom replied, "*there is no distinction between the dharma and your own mind.*"'[64]

In other words, that which occurs in one's own mind is most important of all. Even reading the scriptures or 'practising meditation', when considered as exercises *separate* from life itself, cannot teach as much as paying attention to one's own mind. But when you recognise that in each and every activity you engage in, there is an opportunity for learning and cultivating the mind, then true progress can be made.

---

[64] *Miscellaneous Advice of the Kadampa Masters [from.* Batchelor, 1997, 55]. My Italics.

A 'travel analogy' used in both philosophies makes the same point. As Seneca recalls Socrates' advice on the perils of travelling so as to escape from ourselves ('Why do you wonder that travel abroad does no good, when you carry yourself along? What drove you from home still sticks close,')[65] so too does Thich Nhat Hanh say that, although one might go for a drive when 'we want to get away from ourselves', ultimately 'anywhere we go we will have our self with us'.[66] Our progress in philosophy cannot be separated from our life and from what we are doing at any given moment. Thus, as the followers of Thich Nhat Hanh's Zen Buddhism vow, 'Truth is found in life, and we will observe life within and around us in every moment, ready to learn throughout our lives',[67] so too does Epictetus remind his students 'Never look for your (philosophical) work in one place and your progress in another.'[68] Improving our abilities to live well is not something done in isolation from life: rather it happens precisely in the very nitty-gritty details of the everyday. As Marcus Aurelius writes: 'All things here are just as they would be on a hilltop, or by the seashore, or wherever you choose.'[69]

No escape: just this here, now, over and over again - the philosophical 'training ground' of life. Philosophical practice is not abstract: it is to be found in reality. Wherever you go, there you are.

---

[65] Seneca, *Letters*, 28.1.
[66] 2005a, 70.
[67] *Second Mindfulness Training* [from Thich Nhat Hanh (2005), 92].
[68] *Discourses*, 1.4.17.
[69] Marcus Aurelius, *Meditations*, 10.23.

Tending to the Garden of the Mind: Malleability of Self in Stoicism and Buddhism

With this understanding at base, there develops a responsibility in both philosophies to see the world more skilfully, in ways that are conducive to living an ethical life. That this is considered possible is a result of the second core aspect of psychology I mentioned above on which Stoicism and Buddhism agree, that of the malleability of the self. Rather beautifully, both Stoicism and Buddhism describe the process of self-change as being akin to making a beautiful garden. We can chose to cultivate our minds in beautiful directions, planting seeds of joy, wisdom and understanding that will later bear fruit.

In this way, Thich Nhat Hanh considers that the function of conscious cognition (or as he calls it: 'mind consciousness') is to water positive seeds in the subconscious ('store consciousness') so as to bring about more wholesome states of mind consistently. He writes: 'The store consciousness is often described as the earth - the garden where the seeds that give rise to flowers and fruits are sown. The mind consciousness is the gardener, the one who sows, waters, and takes care of the earth.'[70] Essentially, what is being described here is the fact that, over time, our conscious mind can cultivate more beautiful and skilful mind states which, in turn, leads to changing the subconscious positively. Likewise, Epictetus compares the student's inner development to a fig ripening: 'Let it flower first of all,

---

[70] 2006b, 136.

then bring forth its fruit and then become ripe'.[71] One is consistently seeking to transform unwholesome thoughts and emotions we might have so as to develop a more wholesome mind. The conscious part of us does this - the part which can take a step back, reflect on our emotions, guide our mind in deliberately chosen directions, divert our attention - and each time we do this, we are changing the subconscious origins of our thoughts and emotions.

This is not just a 'nice idea'. Rather, both philosophies consider that we have a *responsibility* to engage in this process of ensuring that we continually encourage the mind in better directions. We should discourage unskilful, and potentially harmful thoughts, from remaining in our mind: our focus should instead be on cultivating the opposite. Thich Nhat Hanh describes this process as 'Fourfold Right Diligence'. They are:

> ' (1) preventing unwholesome seeds in our store consciousness that have not yet arisen from arising, (2) helping the unwholesome seeds that have already arisen to return to our store consciousness, (3) finding ways to water the wholesome seeds in our store consciousness that have not yet arisen..., and (4) nourishing the wholesome seeds that have already arisen so that they will stay present in our mind consciousness and grow stronger.'[72]

In *Discourses* 2.18, we find that Epictetus essentially suggests the exact same method. Selections from that

---

[71] *Discourses*, 1.15.7.
[72] 1998, 100.

Discourse, within the same framework as that of the Fourfold Right Diligence above, will illustrate this:

> ' (1) 'So if you want to be free from a negative passion, don't feed your habit, and present it with nothing to make it grow',[73] (2) '...introduce and set over against it some fair and noble impression and throw out this filthy one,'[74] (3) 'In general, therefore, if you want to do something, make a habit of it'[75] (4) 'If you form the habit of taking such exercises, you will see what mighty shoulders you develop, what sinews, what vigour.'[76]

Both philosophies in this way advocate methods which discourage mental habits identified as unwholesome, change a habit once it has arisen and encourage new and wholesome habits to take root. In this way, there is a constant interplay, as we would understand it today, between the conscious and subconscious minds: we use the conscious mind to change the emotions and impulses that come from our subconscious and, in turn, this will change the kind of thoughts and feelings that arise from the subconscious in the first place. Eventually, we form new habits once the subconscious is changed: we develop 'mighty shoulders' as Epictetus metaphorically puts it.

However, progress does not come quickly or easily. As Epictetus says of this process: 'And if you wish to make an examination of all your own beliefs, this hardly takes just one day, as you know'.[77] So too in Buddhism, there is, as the Buddha says, 'no sudden

---

[73] *Discourses,* 2.18.12.
[74] *Discourses*, 2.18.24-25.
[75] *Discourses*, 2.18. 4.
[76] *Discourses*, 2.16.26.
[77] *Discourses* ,1.11.39-40.

penetration to final knowledge' but instead 'just as the great ocean gradually shelves, slopes and inclines, and there is no sudden precipice, so also in this Dharma and Discipline there is a gradual training, a gradual course, a gradual progression.'[78] Everything is a learning process and, in fact, this process never ends. How we relate to life as it unfolds is a process mind-development, a development which, in turn, strengthens the mind for life as it unfolds. Life is an ongoing project of ethical development until the day we die.

Essential Goodness: A Positive View of the Human Being

But are human beings considered capable of such progress? In this regard, we come to another core similarity in that each approach considers the human to be inherently good, or at least as inherently capable of being good. In Buddhism, this concept of 'original goodness'[79], or the 'inner nobility and beauty of all human beings',[80] is called 'Buddha Nature'. Thich Nhat Hanh describes it as follows: 'The seed of enlightenment is already within our consciousness. This is our Buddha Nature - the inherent quality of enlightened mind that we all possess, and which needs only to be nurtured.'[81] We find the same idea, that of nurturing an inner core of goodness, in Stoicism and in particular in Marcus Aurelius: 'Dig within, for within you lies the

---

[78] *Udana* (*Inspired Utterances*), 5.5 [from Batchelor, *Can. Cit.*, 7].
[79] Jack Kornfield (2008), 12.
[80] Jack Kornfield (2008), 12.
[81] 2006b, 26.

fountain of good, and it can always be gushing forth if only you always dig.'[82] For Epictetus, this theme underpins one's whole understanding of self-identity: the human being is naturally equipped with magnanimity, courage and strength,[83] and has the innate ability to never become 'stuck' in the face of events.[84] The purpose of both philosophies is, in large part, to uncover this innate goodness bit by bit. This positive conception of humanity implies that each of us, no matter what baggage we carry, no matter what our wounds might be, no matter how great our toxic shame, has the potential to find that 'fountain of goodness' which is within us and to cultivate it.

It might sound unrealistic to think that humans have this inherent goodness by nature. Are the Stoics not aware of how malicious we can be? Of the atrocious acts humans can perpetrate towards one another, others species and the planet? Of course, they are. However, the fact that there are those who still continue to act with unwholesome intentions can be attributed to their own woundedness and misplaced values that they have learnt in turn from a wounded society. Indeed, both philosophies agree that most people do not *willingly* act in order to bring about suffering - rather such actions come from deep ignorance about what really matters in life. As Thich Nhat Hanh writes 'We don't want to suffer, but our deep-seated habit energies drag us into the fire of suffering' so too does Epictetus recall Plato's saying

---

[82] *Meditations,* 7.59.
[83] *Discourses*, 1.6.28-29.
[84] *Discourses*, 1.25.3.

that 'every soul is unwillingly deprived of the truth'.[85] On a personal note, I would agree with both Epictetus and Thich Nhat Hanh here with a slight qualification. With the exception of psychopaths, sociopaths and malignant narcissists, for my part I believe that what both Epictetus and Thich Nhat Hanh say in this regard is largely true. The point is that what *really* leads to happiness is not well understood by most, and we need to study the nature of happiness in order to help us uncover our innate qualities of goodness, which, for all kinds of reasons - early trauma, abuse, the narcissistic competitiveness of the very air we breath - may have been covered up. But they are still there, quietly waiting for us to cultivate them.

Non-Dogmatic, Anti-Authoritarian Philosophies

In the introduction, I mentioned that the particular form of Buddhism practised in the West could be considered, in the words of the 12th century monk Yun Men, as 'an appropriate statement.' But the anti-authoritarian spirit of this justification is to be found in Stoicism also. Now, if one delves beneath Stoicism's *seemingly* dogmatic nature (for example their claim that there is an objective and universal way to live which applies to all of us, namely the 'life in accordance with nature'), one begins to perceive a system where individualized applications of the philosophy were encouraged. During one teaching, Epictetus finds himself confronted with the following request from a

---

[85] *Discourses*, 1.28.4. This saying was originally found in Plato, *Sophists*, 228c.

student: 'But just tell me what to do!' Epictetus' response gets to the heart of that which the scholar Martha Nussbaum has termed the Stoic streak of 'anti-authoritarianism.'[86] As Epictetus makes clear, all the work must be done by the student, not by the teacher:

> '...Bring forth your preconceptions, bring forth what you have learnt from the philosophers, bring forth what you have often heard, bring forth what you have said yourself, bring forth what you have read yourself, bring forth what you have practised yourself.'[87]

We read philosophy in order to live philosophy. Epictetus reminds his students that treading philosophical books is *not* the point: he uses the metaphorical example of wanting evidence of strong shoulders and not of the weights used to strengthen them.[88] Previous Stoic teachers are to be respected but not blindly believed. Virtue is not the reading of Chrysippus,[89] one of the earliest heads of the Stoic school, rather, his texts are only required in so far as he describes the philosophy's core tenets.[90] Epictetus promises to send anyone caught *only* reading philosophy books, neglectful of applying the principles in their home-life, straight back home again in order 'not to neglect matters there'.[91] This anti-authoritarian, wholly pragmatic, spirit is perhaps most incisively expressed by Seneca. Consider these two passages:

---

[86] 1996, 344-348.
[87] *Discourses*, 1.25.6.
[88] *Discourses*, 1.4.13.
[89] *Discourses*, 1.4.7
[90] *Discourses*, 1.17.18.
[91] *Discourses*, 1.4.22.

> 'We are not subjects of a (philosophical) monarch; every individual asserts his freedom.'[92]

> '...how long will you march under another man's orders...put some distance between you and your books. How long will you be a student? From now on, be a teacher as well.'[93]

All in all, this means that the philosophy's practical applications must evolve. Seneca further writes: 'if we rest content with solutions offered, the real solution will never be found.'[94] In this way, Stoicism emphasises, as does Western Buddhism also, placing power in the hands of the practitioner. Batchelor's statement that Buddhist practice '...no longer requires the support of moralistic rules and religious ritual; it is grounded in integrity and creative autonomy'[95] describes an innovative spirit, one that we also find in Stoicism. Speaking of Chrysippus and his status among later Stoics, the scholar of Stoicism Anthony Long writes:

> 'It is true that Chrysippus' writings acquired canonical status, but this did not oblige the Late Stoics to become his clones or to give up thinking for themselves.'[96]

What is the result of this? In a word: *autarkeia* (the Greek for 'self-sufficiency'). One learns to see for oneself what is the best and most appropriate application of the teachings. This very spirit of self-sufficiency and of anti-authoritarianism, of not being tied in a rigid way to previous strands of the

---

[92] Seneca, *Letters* 33.4.
[93] Seneca, *Letters* 33.7-9.
[94] Seneca, *Letters* 33. 10.
[95] 1997, 9.
[96] 2002, 19.

philosophy, informs the *Modern Stoicism* movement and the evolution of Stoicism that is ongoing today. Real philosophy as a way of life is dynamic: there may indeed be a strong sense of the pre-existing 'answers' the philosophy provides, but these shift and respond to the rapidly changing circumstances of our world. This involves a complex relationship between respectfully sifting through deeply thought out responses to life which have been 'passed down' through history and intelligently engaging with these responses given our advancements in human understanding and also taking into account our own life circumstances and the wisdom we have acquired so far in our own journey.

Conclusion

In this chapter, I have considered some overall similarities in philosophical attitude and approach which Stoicism and Buddhism share. Both systems agree we need to focus on finding a 'flourishing' response to life within its harsh realities, and that there is a way of training the mind and living with virtue and ethics that can allow us to do that. Both philosophies also believe that the human being is inherently capable of goodness and that this can be 'uncovered' through philosophical practice, and that this is possible as the self is malleable: it can change, slowly but surely, in wiser directions.

But how does this change occur in a practical way? What is the Stoic or Buddhist actually doing on a day-to-day basis which changes the self?

Let us now turn to consider the central role of 'mindfulness' in both Stoicism and Buddhism.

Chapter Two

Mindfulness in Stoicism & Buddhism

A philosophy that is concerned with self-change needs techniques and tools which are focussed on developing *awareness* of character, an awareness which subsequently allows for change of character. For we are not dealing, as the scholar of Stoicism Pierre Hadot writes, with a case '...of mere knowledge, but with the transformation of our personality.'[97] There are so many aspects of Stoicism and of Buddhism that one could discuss in this regard, but I wish to focus in particular on the one central discipline which allows, in both philosophies, for self-change to occur on a moment to moment basis, that of 'mindfulness'.

Most know of 'mindfulness' today as a form of meditation and way of focussing on some aspect of the present moment which stems from Buddhist practice. But the Stoics also had an analogous kind of practice, which they called, in Ancient Greek, *'prosoche'*. This means 'attention', but we can helpfully translate it as 'mindfulness', given that it contains noticeable similarities to the Buddhist version.

---

[97] 1995, 84.

In this chapter, I will explore Stoic and Buddhist mindfulness in several key ways. First, I shall talk about how both philosophies encourage an attentiveness to the present moment, particularly so as to encourage ethical transformation. Then I shall discuss how we can helpfully think of Stoicism and Buddhism as being akin to forms of Cognitive Behavioural Therapy (C.B.T.), although there are important differences between C.B.T. and both philosophies. And, finally, I will consider the main differences and similarities between Buddhist meditation practices and Stoic spiritual exercises. Considering these three areas will give us an idea of what it means to practice both of these philosophies on a day to day basis.

Ethical Attention to the Present Moment

As Marcus Aurelius reminds himself that each man only lives in this present moment ('That each man only lives in this present instant...all the rest either has been lived or remains in uncertainty'),[98] so too does Thich Nhat Hanh remind his reader '...to be aware that we are here and now, and the only moment to be alive is the present moment.'[99] So far, so similar, but do both philosophies focus their attention on the present moment in the same way?

In Western Buddhism, emphasis on the present moment is often seen as an opportunity to see the world with 'fresh eyes', along with an 'opening of the senses.'[100] The Buddhist practitioner learns to bring

---

[98] *Meditations*, 3.10.
[99] 2005a, 16.
[100] McMahan, 216.

her attention to the level of sensation, and, with the conceptual mind at rest, many otherwise normal phenomena can be seen as a 'miracle'.[101] This kind of practice is about sensing the *aliveness* of each moment, fully aware of, for example, a leaf falling or the breeze blowing. It is described by Thich Nhat Hanh as entering the 'world of reality,'[102] and occurs when the process of experiencing the world through our own (inner-verbal) assessments is temporarily at rest. This kind of present moment focus will be familiar to many who practise mindfulness in its most contemporary forms.

I do not think that the Stoics had an equivalent 'Zen-like' simplicity, or at least it seems to me that they did not cultivate this as a deliberate philosophical practice (although, of course, an appreciation for life 'beyond words' at certain moments of profound joy, in recognising the beauty of nature for example, could certainly be a part of Stoicism). Rather, as we shall see shortly, I think the focus on the present moment in Stoicism is given high importance primarily as it represents the principal opportunity for us to practise virtue. In this way, the present moment is a moment which is imbued with rich ethical potential. Are Stoicism and Western Buddhism to part ways, therefore, when it comes to 'mindfulness'?

Far from it. Indeed, the conception of mindfulness in Western Buddhism is much vaster than the basic idea of a non-conceptual appreciation of the present moment which I described above, as it too also encourages a kind of ethical and discerning use of the

---

[101] McMahan, 216.
[102] 1975, 12.

present. Indeed, in both Stoicism and Buddhism, mindfulness has a purpose and, we could say, an 'enlightened agenda'. For, by becoming more aware, in particular of our emotions and thoughts, we learn skilful ways to encourage self-transformation. In doing so, we are engaging in changing the self in an ethical direction: we are realising our values. For the Buddha, developing mindfulness was essential in that it became the means for '...living beings to realize purification, overcome directly grief and sorrow, end pain and anxiety, travel the right path, and realize nirvana.'[103] For Epictetus, the person who is *inattentive* to life is '...putting off from one time to another tranquil and appropriate living, the life in accordance with nature, and persistence in that life.'[104] As the scholar Pierre Hadot elaborates, '...the fundamental attitude that the Stoic must maintain at each instant of his life is one of attention...concentrated upon each and every moment, in order not to miss anything which is contrary to reason.'[105] In Stoicism, attention to the moment is precisely what allows us to practice virtue.

In both philosophies, developing 'mindfulness' is therefore seen as an essential part of realizing the path, that is *living in accordance with nature* as in the case of Stoicism or pursuing *the cessation of suffering* as in the case of Buddhism. This is not just about a profound, sub-conceptual appreciation of the moment. Rather, the cultivation of 'mindfulness' also results in the

---

[103] *Majjhima Nikaya* (*The Middle Length Discourses*) in Thich Nhat Hanh (2006a), 13.
[104] *Discourses* 4.12.2.
[105] 1995, 226.

cultivation of a steady, ethically focussed mind. As the *Dhammapada* states: 'Not a mother, not a father will do so much, nor any other relatives; a well-directed mind will do us greater service.'[106] Likewise, Epictetus reminds his students that a mind that is not attentive easily loses its sense of direction towards that which is wholesome: 'Do you not realize that when once you have let your mind go wandering, it is no longer in your power to recall it, to bring it to bear upon either seemliness, or self-respect, or moderation?'[107] Anyone who puts this practice off until tomorrow, Epictetus says, is essentially saying to the world that: 'Today, I will be shameless, tactless, abject; it will be in the power of other men to make me grieve; I will get angry today, I will give way to envy.'[108] Without mindfulness, we can live so easily on an 'autopilot' that will lead us in directions we may regret.

In short, mindfulness, in both traditions, is the means by which the application of ethical ideas becomes real. That this should be the case is because of the sense that it is only *now*, in the present moment, that the 'material' of life can be shaped well. In Stoicism, the emphasis is placed on guiding the present moment in the direction of virtue. As Marcus Aurelius writes: '...concerning yourself with the present alone, guide that to holiness and justice...',[109] and, for Marcus, this is an act which will allow the future to look after itself: 'Do not allow the future to trouble your mind; for

---

[106] *Dhammapada*, 43.
[107] *Discourses,* 4.12.6.
[108] *Discourses* 4.12. 20.
[109] *Meditations,* 12.1.

you will come to it, if come you must, bringing with you the same reason that you now apply to the affairs of the present'.[110] In Buddhism, the same thought is found. The fourty-seventh verse of Thich Nhat Hanh's *Verses on the Nature of Consciousness* goes as follows:

> 'The present moment / contains past and future. / The secret of transformation / is the way we handle this very moment.'[111]

The here and now is most important because of how we relate to it from an ethical standpoint, knowing that living well *now* actually means both healing the past and preparing for the future.

And it is not just that we can become more aware of patterns of thought and emotion through mindfulness, but also that we can perform our daily activities in such a way that we are living with dignity and ethically. This could include many things we do everyday, and particularly those activities which would not necessarily strike one as 'spiritual'. All the 'small things' in life are done better, Epictetus says, with an attentive mind,[112] and, for Thich Nhat Hanh, similarly, everything we do carries a significance:

> 'Each act is a rite, a ceremony...Does the word "rite" seem too solemn? I use that word in order to jolt you into the realization of the life-and-death matter of awareness.'[113]

---

[110] *Meditations,* 7.8.
[111] 2006b, 229. These verses were originally written by a Buddhist scholar, Vasubandhu, who lived in the fourth and fifth centuries AD and Thich Nhat Hanh later reworked them.
[112] *Discourses*, 4.12.5.
[113] 1975, 24.

In light of this, bathing and eating, for example, are just as much a part of the philosophical path as anything else. During such activities, Thich Nhat Hanh recommends reciting a series of *gathas* ('short verses designed to focus a person's mind on the activity of the moment').[114] In this way, while washing, the practitioner can recite 'Rinsing my body / my heart is cleansed,'[115] a kind of purification ritual reminding him or her to continue leading an ethical life. Similarly, the second contemplation of Thich Nhat Hanh's *The Five Contemplations for Mindful Eating*[116] is: 'May we eat with mindfulness and gratitude so as to be worthy to receive this food.' Both of these practices chime with Epictetus' own advice to his students to bathe as a faithful man and to eat as a humble man:[117] faithful, because of a sense of certainty in the life of virtue; humble, because temperance in food is training for temperance in life. In these ways, both Stoicism and Buddhism encourage us to make otherwise mundane activities part of our philosophical path.

What I hope the above discussion to have shown is that, in both traditions, their approach to what might be termed as 'mindfulness' contains a very strong and primary ethical dimension. In fact, tendencies (which do exist) among Buddhists not to realize that mindfulness practice is inextricably linked with ethics are strongly discouraged by, for example, Thich Nhat Hanh. He writes that he knows '…some Zen students who think that they

---

[114] King (2001), 72.
[115] 2006c, 23.
[116] 2006c, 67.
[117] *Discourses*, 1.4.20.

can practice meditation without practicing precepts, but that is not correct. The heart of Buddhist meditation is the practice of precepts, and mindfulness is the practice of the precepts,'[118] elaborating further that 'When Right Mindfulness is present, the Four Noble Truths and the seven other elements of the Eightfold Path are also present.'[119] Having said this, I myself think that a deep non-conceptual appreciation of the wonders of the moment is also ethical. Indeed, to derive delight in the simplicities of the moment, in an age when we are forced by society to find our happiness in an imagined future of material success, is surely itself an ethical choice.

In conclusion, a far greater similarity emerges between both systems than we might have thought at first. While there is no deliberate cultivation of a sub-conceptual 'Zen-like' appreciation of the moment in Stoicism, it does recommend the intertwining of an ethical awareness with the present moment, an intertwining which Buddhism, including Western Buddhism, also recommends. Regarding mindfulness in both traditions, we can conclude: ethics first, present moment appreciation second.

Stoic and Buddhist Cognitive Behavioural Therapy

> 'Stay with me a little while, sense-impression (*phantasia*). Allow me to see who you are and from where you come. Allow me to examine you.'[120] - Epictetus

---

[118] 1998, 82.
[119] 1998, 64.
[120] *Discourses,* 2.18.24.

> 'Breathing in / I know that an unpleasant feeling has just arisen in me...Breathing out/ I can see the roots of this unpleasant feeling.'[121]
>
> 'Hello, Fear. There you are again.'[122] - Thich Nhat Hanh

Both philosophies encourage a healthy sense of doubt towards the thoughts and emotions we have each and every day. The aim of this doubt is to encourage us to take a step back when we have certain thoughts or feelings, examine them, and come up with a 'wise response' to them.

One such 'wise response' is simply to ensure that we have an accurate conception of what has occurred, and that we are not 'clouded' by, for example, erroneous thinking or overwhelming emotions. For, it is not, as Epictetus says, '...the things themselves that disturb men, but their judgements about these things',[123] a psychological basis echoed by Thich Nhat Hanh when he writes that '...wrong perceptions cause incorrect thinking and unnecessary suffering,'[124] encouraging his students instead to ask themselves continuously, 'are you sure?'[125]

This focus on maintaining accuracy in our thoughts and emotions might seem rather similar to 'Cognitive Behavioural Therapy' (C.B.T.), a therapy designed for the removal of harmful beliefs which lead to, and perpetuate, various mental health problems, including anxiety disorders. C.B.T. in particular focuses on how *accurate* our thoughts and feelings may be.

---

[121] 2006a, 58ff. Text modified [original = 'pleasant' feeling, but this method is applicable to all feelings].
[122] 1995, 66.
[123] *Handbook* §5..
[124] 1998, 61.
[125] 1998, 60-61.

Indeed, Stoicism and Buddhism are often regarded as being akin to C.B.T. in that both philosophies engage in actively replacing thoughts and behaviours, and, in that sense, both philosophies are, in a sense, forms of cognitive and behavioural therapy in their own right. Furthermore, it has been argued that both philosophies influenced the development of C.B.T. In the case of Stoicism, Albert Ellis, the founder of C.B.T., cited Epictetus and Marcus Aurelius as some of his main inspirations,[126] and Donald Robertson, a member of the *Modern Stoicism* project, has written a book on the Stoic origins of C.B.T.[127] Meanwhile, in the case of Buddhism, Albert Ellis also cited the Buddha as one of his inspirations and, interestingly, Jack Kornfield considers that Buddhists were the '...first cognitive-behavioural therapists.'[128] He cites the Buddha's words from the *Vitakkasanthana Sutta* (*Discourse on Removing Distracting Thoughts*) from the *Majhima Nikaya* (*The Middle Length Discourses*) in support of this:

> 'There is the case where evil, unskilful thoughts - imbued with desire, aversion, or delusion arise...(and then) he (the monk) should attend to another theme, apart from that one, connected with what is skilful....just as a skilled carpenter or his apprentice would use a small peg to knock out, drive out and pull out a large one...'[129]

---

[126] In an interview with J. Evans (http://philosophyforlife.org/albert-ellis-on-philosophy-as-therapy/)
[127] *The Philosophy of CBT: Stoic Philosophy as Rational and Cognitive Psychotherapy,* Karnac, 2010.
[128] 2008, 293.
[129] *Majhima Nikaya*, I.119.

Such a 'thought-replacement' exercise is clearly a kind of cognitive therapy and we find something very similar in Stoicism with its emphasis on replacing 'initial thoughts' we have with wiser and more virtuous thoughts. However, while these general similarities do exist, it is very important, in my view, to separate both Buddhism and Stoicism from the more 'clinical' and overly rationalistic nature of C.B.T., even though there may be some similarities. For, ultimately, Stoicism and Buddhism are philosophies which seek to offer coherent frameworks for life as a whole, something which C.B.T. does not, and cannot ever, do. C.B.T. focuses on removing specific problems, and it can be very helpful with this, but does not offer a 'bigger picture' approach for understanding life and how to live in general.

Let us consider instead the nature of Stoic and Buddhist behaviourism in their own right. If we were to categorise Buddhism or Stoicism as a form of C.B.T., how would we describe them? And what kind of practices in daily life would these philosophies encourage?

Buddhist 'Behaviourism With Heart'

In the case of Buddhism, Kornfield terms Buddhism's equivalent to C.B.T. as 'Behaviourism with Heart,'[130] writing that one changes thoughts out of compassion for oneself and others,[131] and that this is what is in '...our genuine interest,'[132] thereby divorcing the

---

[130] Kornfield (2008), 293.
[131] Kornfield (2008), 296
[132] Kornfield (2008), 299.

practice from a more clinical-therapeutic context. Rather than purely changing thoughts or emotions in order to make them more 'accurate', the Buddhist is also interested in cultivating a heart-felt response to our emotions and to those of others. Compassion is the 'reference point' to which the Buddhist so often refers in working with her thoughts and emotions. When we have feelings, particularly ones that we might otherwise try to avoid, the Buddhist instead aims to accept them, with a gentle and understanding love, and, in general, the Buddhist seeks solutions to larger life problems by considering them in the most compassionate light possible.

This encapsulates the heart of a Buddhist's daily practice. The focus is on using mindfulness to accept the emotional flow of the day with a gentle love. This compassionate awareness allows the self to change gradually.

Stoic 'Behaviourism Towards Virtue'

But what would the equivalent be in Stoicism? I would suggest that the Stoic equivalent is 'Behaviourism towards Virtue'. By this I mean that the Stoic tries continuously to work out how to reframe their emotions and thoughts in light of virtue, which, according to Stoicism, is the most important thing in life.

Let us consider the following passage from Marcus Aurelius which essentially captures how this process works:

> '...always make a sketch or plan of whatever presents itself to your mind, so as to see what sort of thing it is when stripped down to its essence, as

a whole and in its separate parts; and tell yourself its proper name, and the names of the elements from which it has been put together and into which it will finally be resolved. For nothing is as effective in creating greatness of mind as being able to examine methodically and truthfully everything that presents itself in life, and always viewing things in such a way as to consider what kind of use each thing serves in what kind of universe, and what value it has to human beings as citizens of the highest of cities…and what this object is that presently makes an impression on me, and what it is composed of, and how long it will naturally persist, and what virtue is needed in the face of it, such as gentleness, courage, truthfulness, good faith, simplicity, self-sufficiency, and so forth.'[133]

What Marcus suggests here is the cultivation of clear awareness of thoughts, and this involves taking a step back so as to delineate clearly what is on one's mind. Marcus then tries to discern what place these thoughts and feelings might have in relation to his own ethical beliefs about what is most important in life. What kind of value-judgements are 'packed into' these impressions and are they ethically helpful? Then, he wishes to work out which ethical qualities will be of most help in approaching the situation to which the impressions relate: will it, for example, be gentleness, courage, or simplicity? This in particular is the point at which the Stoic tries to work out the 'virtuous response' to the impressions under consideration. Indeed, the entire purpose of the exercise is one of increasing ethical awareness. As Chris Gill, a scholar on Stoicism, writes of this passage: 'Although this may seem at first to be a

---

[133] *Meditations*, 3.11.

purely scientific or analytical procedure, what Marcus has in mind is getting to the *ethical* core of the situation.'[134] By following these steps, Marcus takes the thoughts and feelings that arise in his mind and reframes them in the light of Stoic virtue. And, then, once he acts based upon his 'virtuous response', he will have successfully modified his behaviour 'towards virtue'.

How can we sum up both approaches in the light of the C.B.T. analogy? The Buddhist continually moulds himself towards the compassionate mind. Indeed, Thich Nhat Hanh explains that the Chinese character for 'mindfulness' contains the signs for both 'now' and 'heart.'[135] The Stoic, in contrast, consistently strives to mould her character towards virtue. If Stoic '*prosoche*/mindfulness' had a Chinese character, it would be the signs for 'now' and 'virtue'.

Buddhist Meditation Practices and Stoic 'Spiritual Exercises'

> '…It is possible for you to retreat into yourself whenever you please; for nowhere can one retreat into greater peace or freedom from care than within one's own soul…'[136] - Marcus Aurelius

> 'It is a joy to sit, stable and at ease, and return to ourselves - our breathing, our half smile, …our true nature.'[137] - Thich Nhat Hanh

Let us start with the similarities. It is clear that Marcus Aurelius did set aside periods for formal reflection,

---

[134] 2011, xvii.
[135] 1998, 64f.
[136] *Meditations,* 11.19.
[137] 2006c, 32.

periods which he encouraged himself to maintain regularly so as to renew himself.[138] The Greek word he uses for such an activity is 'anachoresis' which quite literally means 'returning within' and which is thus most often translated as 'retreat'. During this time, it seems that Marcus would bring to mind, and reflect upon, simple and elemental Stoic axioms, or short sayings which encapsulated key Stoic ideas. The scholar Pierre Hadot considers that reducing the complexities of Stoic philosophy to such axioms was essential in allowing for its 'fundamental principles' to '…remain easily accessible to the mind, and be applicable with the sureness and constancy of reflex.'[139] In the context of the inner 'retreat', Marcus gives the example of saying this phrase to himself:

'The Universe is change, Life is Opinion'.[140]

By inwardly reciting this expression, Marcus intends to remind himself of the core Stoic tenets of impermanence, and of the fact that one's life is determined by one's perceptions, that is to say, by what one thinks and not by externals. Such a practice is intended to renew his commitment to the philosophical path, acting as a restorative activity in so far as it allows for the affairs in his life to be put into perspective. Marcus further presents this 'retreat' as a return to *his own little plot of land*.[141] This time of retreat is meant to be a time of cultivation and of development.

---

[138] *Discourses*, 4.3.1.
[139] 1995, 84.
[140] *Discourses*, 4.3.4.
[141] *Discourses*, 4.3.4.

The most analogous Buddhist practice, found in the approach of Thich Nhat Hanh, involves the unification of awareness of the breath with *gathas*, short phrases which aim to bring one's awareness to some aspect of the present moment experience (interestingly, in a way which recalls Marcus' retreat to his own metaphorical 'plot of land', it is often presented as a return to the 'Island of the Self').[142] There are numerous *gathas* the Buddhist might recite, but an illustrative practice is the following:

> 'Breathing in, I calm my body / Breathing out, I smile. / Dwelling in the present moment / I know this is a wonderful moment.'[143]

This is a (deceptively) simple practice which actually encourages the practitioner in a similar direction to Marcus: awareness of the 'wonders' of the present moment is possible precisely because those wonders are *impermanent*, while the decision to smile is seen as making you 'master of yourself',[144] and not, one could say, *controlled by external events*.

In both cases, the act of retreat is perceived, once again, as an ethical preparation for the rest of life: it is certainly not an 'escape' from life. Rather, Marcus explicitly states that he engages in this reflection so as to leave him '...with no discontent to those affairs to which you return,'[145] and, similarly, Thich Nhat Hanh writes that his 'main concern' is '...the effect the gatha has on the non-gatha state of mind',[146] further

---

[142] Thich Nhat Hanh (2009), 13.
[143] Thich Nhat Hanh (2006c), 32.
[144] Thich Nhat Hanh (2005a), 15.
[145] *Discourses,* 4.3.1.
[146] 2005a, 60.

elaborating that even '...one gatha...will influence the rest of the day.'[147] In this sense both systems agree on the ethical nature of meditation, and how a 'retreat' is most helpful for the more 'active' hours of the day. The periods of meditation are akin to a 'breath in' and a preparation for the more engaged parts of the day which can be considered a 'breath out'.

However, the actual process of other meditative exercises notably differs in form between the two philosophies. For a start, reciting Stoic *axioms* inwardly was but one practice. Many other Stoic spiritual exercises were highly reflective and conceptual (as is evidenced from the form of Marcus' own written reflections, *The Meditations*, which were all essentially a philosophical exercise for himself). Furthermore, Stoic spiritual exercises were often either prospective or retrospective in orientation, while the Buddhist's meditation practice most often (though by no means always) centres on cultivating greater attention of some aspect of the *here and now* on the level of sensation. This difference is nowhere more clearly illustrated than with the Buddhist emphasis on cultivating *awareness of the breath* in sitting meditation. Focussing on the breath is seen as important for developing *samadhi* ('calm abiding'),[148] reducing the mind's tendency for dispersal, and is, as Thich Nhat Hanh writes, essential in that: 'If you do not have enough concentration, you cannot be strong enough to have an insight into a subject of your

---

[147] 2005a, 60.
[148] Thich Nhat Hanh (2006a), 37.

meditation.'[149] For this and other reasons, a Buddhist practises 'mindfulness of breathing' during sitting meditation, a dedicated period of time to develop concentration and insight into the workings of the mind. Furthermore, emphasis is placed on the quality of the breath ('our in-breaths and out-breaths should flow smoothly and lightly') and of the impact of this on the state of mind of the practitioner ('...the more subtle our breath is, the more peaceful our body and mind will be.')[150] There is no equivalent of this in Stoicism.

In addition, this difference becomes more evident when other mindfulness practices are considered. For the recitation of *gathas*, although clearly involving some level of conceptualization along with awareness of the breath, is a practice particular to the approach of Thich Nhat Hanh. For example, the 'Insight Meditation' tradition (of which Jack Kornfield is a member) focusses more on the cultivation of *awareness* itself, emphasizing its capacity to hold thoughts and emotions with kindness and without reactivity. Kornfield defines mindfulness in this instance as '...a non-judging and respectful awareness...(which)...does not reject experience. It lets experience be the teacher.'[151] This kind of meditation can hold the breath as the main object of awareness, but *without* any deliberate conceptual thought: there are no *gathas* in this approach. Thoughts, emotions and bodily sensations will take the mind's attention away from the breath (our mind's ability to pay attention is compared to

---

[149] 2005a, 112.
[150] Thich Nhat Hanh (2006a), 39.
[151] 2008, 96, 101.

monkeys in the ancient Buddhist texts, puppies in the modern ones!),[152] which will occupy the practitioner's attention until her mind registers that her object of attention, for the moment, is meant to be the sensation of the breath. Having noted what was on her mind with the same kindly awareness, she then returns her attention to the sensations of the breath, thereby developing concentration.[153] During this process, awareness of the content of certain thought patterns is increased such that, over time, unskilful thought patterns can be let go of and skilful patterns cultivated instead.[154] And with greater levels of concentration, the mind can be more easily directed in skilful directions.[155] McMahan explains this process as follows:

> '...one first observes the mind in a detached way, noting and sometimes labelling thoughts as they arise; then, through gaining greater familiarity with the mind's patterns, beliefs and habitual emotional responses, one can gain control over the process and acquire insight into the true nature of the process itself, thereby transforming it.'[156]

This kind of experiential exploration of the mind is not found in Stoicism. One could say, therefore, that meditation practices in Buddhism are concerned with every aspect of experience, both at the level of sensation and at the level of the conceptual mind, whereas the Stoic is concerned primarily with the latter. Perhaps a Stoic would find Buddhist practices a helpful aid to his own 'bigger picture' approach, in that

---

[152] Gunaratana (2002), 155.
[153] Jack Kornfield (2008), 107-109.
[154] Jack Kornfield (2008), 141-143.
[155] Jack Kornfield (2008), 323-325.
[156] 2008, 202-203.

they serve to increase awareness of the mind's patterns, while the Buddhist would perhaps consider it useful to take some time to cultivate a 'bigger picture' awareness of events in her life *at the moment* rather than *in this moment.*

Conclusion

Overall, significant differences in method do exist when it comes meditative practice and spiritual exercises. This is unsurprising, however, when one considers that the Buddhist techniques, even in Western Buddhism, must remain Eastern in origin. However, we should note McMahan when he writes that '...what is ironic about the use of Buddhist mindfulness techniques to approach more skilfully the complex vicissitudes of modern life - work, family, social, and political life - is that these techniques were originally developed by monks who had ostensibly renounced these very things.'[157] In that sense, the *spirit* with which the Western Buddhist approaches his periods of meditation is the same as that of the Stoic who also has to engage in family life, work and society at large. Both philosophies share the idea that periods of meditation or reflection serve as a preparation for the contributions we make to society.

There is also the sense, in both philosophies, that thought needs to be well guarded. The life and death nature of awareness, as mentioned by Thich Nhat Hanh earlier, is echoed in Epictetus' recommendation that the Stoic should, from the moment he wakes up, keep

---

[157] 2008, 218.

watch and be on his guard and apply his principles to whatever situation arises.[158] But perhaps more importantly for the overall process, there is the clear sense that the thoughts presented to the mind do *not* define the individual. Instead, the individual regards himself as an ethical awareness or, one could say, an 'ethical self'. This approach emphasizes knowing which thoughts are useful, and which are not, and, on the basis of this, also emphasizes the ability of shaping the self appropriately. The scholar of Stoicism Anthony Long and then Kornfield illustrate this point well:

> 'We are not autonomous over the mere occurrence of impressions…what is up to us is how we interpret such information, and the truth and value we attribute to it.'[159]

> 'Unhealthy thoughts can chain us to the past. They arise as *Vipaka*, the result of past karma that we cannot change. We can, however, change our destructive thoughts in the present.'[160]

In this way the Stoic and the Buddhist are each able to approach their mind with a certain degree of freedom: earlier thought patterns might remain but one need not be *defined* by them: instead there is always the possibility of moving in an ethical and wholesome direction. As I hope to have shown in this chapter, the Stoic and the Buddhist, are free, at least to an impactful degree, to *create* the self. As Batchelor writes: 'By attending to the details of this present moment, by choosing not to recollect the past or plan for the future, you are engaged in a process of *creating yourself* in a

---

[158] *Discourses,* 1.4.20.
[159] 2002, 211.
[160] 2008, 304.

specific and deliberate way.'[161] In light of our discussion, it is clear that there is no place, in Stoicism or Buddhism, for considering everyday life as in any way mundane or monotonous. Rather every day life, the 'otherwise ordinary', *is* the path.

---

[161] 1997, 71.

Chapter Three

Cultivating Compassion

'Like the vine that produces its grapes, seeking nothing more once it has given forth its fruit....so the good man having done one deed well, does not shout it about, but turns to the next good deed, just like the vine turns to bear forth its fruit in due season.'

Marcus Aurelius, *Meditations*, 5.6.

'Even when I do things for the sake of others
No sense of amazement or conceit arises
It is just like feeding myself
I hope for nothing in return.'

Shantideva,
The Way of the Bodhisattva, 8: 116.[162]

Stoicism and Buddhism inspire us to live in a kind of 'altruistic flow' and suggest that the highest forms of happiness that anyone can find come, paradoxically, when we 'forget' ourselves and focus on others.

However, both the Buddha and Zeno, the founder of Stoicism, also said things which seem to strike a different note:

---

[162] From Batchelor (1997), 84.

> 'Having traversed all quarters with the mind, one finds no one anywhere dearer than oneself...'[163] - Buddha

> '...the first and dearest object to every living being is its own existence and its consciousness of that existence.'[164] - Zeno

Both of these quotations emphasise the importance of care for the self. How, then, are selfless acts so very central to the life of goodness in both Stoicism and Buddhism?

The Relationship Between Concern for Self and Compassion for Others

There are several ways which both Buddhism and Stoicism essentially share which can show us why a concern for self, when understood correctly, can naturally lead to compassion for others.

Firstly, that one considers oneself dearest of all is not, of course, a psychological basis which *only* carries importance for oneself. For all *other* human beings also feel the same way about themselves. Let us complete the quotation of the Buddha above: 'Each person holds himself most dear; *hence one who loves himself should not harm others.*' Likewise, Cicero tells us, when describing Stoicism, that the '...mere fact that someone is a man makes it incumbent on another man not to regard him as alien.'[165] If we truly understand our own need for self-care, we will not harm others, for

---

[163] *Samyutta Nikaya* (*The Kindred Sayings*), 3:8.
[164] Diogenes Laertius, *Life of Zeno*, 52.
[165] Cicero, *On Ends,* 3.63.

everyone is in the same, human situation. There is a shared principle of humanity at play.

Secondly, there is the need to find what is the *best* way to live given what kind of nature we, as human beings, have. For the Stoics, we are social beings and, as a result, virtue is inherently social: it becomes most 'active' when we act out of concern for others. In this way, by following virtue, we fulfil our social nature. Epictetus encapsulates this idea as follows:

> '...Zeus has prepared the nature of the rational animal such that he can achieve none of his own proper goods unless he also offers something to the common interest.'[166]

We are 'made', biologically speaking, by Nature (here referred to by Epictetus as 'Zeus' who, as a divine principle which permeated all living creatures, was synonymous with 'Nature' in Stoicism), to find what is best for *us* when we engage with *others*. In Stoicism, the 'self' is an inherently *social self*, not an isolated entity. What is good for me is what is good for me *as a social being*.

This idea goes even further in Stoicism for they suggest that, not only are we all social beings, but also that we are all 'limbs' in the body of humanity. And if each of us is a 'limb' in the body of humanity, then by contributing to the common good, we are contributing to the whole of which we are a part. 'We were born', says Marcus, 'to work together, just like feet, hands, eyelids, the rows of upper and lower teeth,'[167] writing, furthermore, that he considered himself '...a limb of the

---

[166] *Discourses*, 1.19.13-14.
[167] *Meditations*, 2.1.

common body formed by all rational beings.'[168] Similarly, Epictetus writes that the wise man '...knows that from god have descended the seeds of being, not only to his father or grandfather, but to all things born and engendered on the earth.'[169] Ultimately, this understanding encompasses all of humanity, regardless of nationality or race. In practice, this means that we see working for the common good of humanity as being akin to a hand working for the common good of the body. Epictetus describes the kind of attitude this idea instils in us as follows:

> 'To treat nothing as a matter of private profit, not to plan about anything as though a detached unit, but to act like the foot or the hand, which, if they had the faculty of reason and understood the constitution of nature, would never exercise choice or desire in any other way but by reference to the whole.'[170]

In Buddhism, there is a similar idea to that of having a 'social self'. This is the idea of 'interrelationship' and it stems, in particular, from Thich Nhat Hanh. In one of his poems, he writes:

> 'You are me, and I am you.
> Isn't it obvious that we "inter-are"?
> You cultivate the flower in yourself,
> so that I will be beautiful.
> I transform the garbage in myself,
> so that you will not have to suffer.'[171]

---

[168] *Meditations.* 7.13.
[169] *Discourses,* 1.1.4.
[170] *Discourses,* 2.10.4.
[171] 1999, 154.

No one acts in an 'vacuum': all of our deeds affect others in some way, even if only in a small way. This is just a fact of cause and effect. As such, in Buddhism, we are automatically bound up in a chain of events which has consequences for others and, as such, we 'inter-are' with each other. As the self is an inherently *social* self in Stoicism, so too in Buddhism is the self an inherently *interconnected* one. We are not isolated automatons, but rather social beings automatically linked to others.

This Buddhist idea of 'inter-relationship' is also connected to the Buddhist idea of 'Interbeing'. McMahan, a scholar on Buddhism in its most contemporary forms, describes the Interbeing 'formula' as '...any X is made of wholly non X elements.'[172] In this light, Thich Nhat Hanh describes how a piece of paper cannot exist without non-paper elements. One could summarize his explanation of this as follows:

> *This paper needs trees, therefore it also needs rain, therefore it also needs clouds. This paper needs a logger, therefore it also needs food for the logger, therefore it also needs a mother for the logger. All of these elements also need sunshine in order to exist at all.*[173]

He concludes his discussion by writing that 'As thin as this sheet of paper is, it contains everything in the universe in it.'[174] This is a new Buddhist idea and unique to Western Buddhism. However, one can see how the Buddhist concept of 'Anatta', or the lack of a fixed *inherent* existence in anything, and 'Interdependent Co-origination', or the concept of 'this is because

---

[172] 2008, 174.
[173] 1995, 95-96.
[174] 1995, 96.

that is', have led to this new theory: nothing in the world exists, in this view, as a wholly separate entity.

And, importantly, this includes us humans and, as such, has implications for how we understand ourselves and how we relate to others. The individual is no longer just an individual but is also made up of 'non-individual' elements. In light of this, one can see each human being as being part of a much larger causal web of life, in a way similar (if not quite the same) to how the Stoic thinks of himself as a limb in the common body of humanity.

But, in practice, this idea of 'interbeing', can lead the Buddhist also to feel as if they are a 'limb' in the body of humankind. Indeed, Thich Nhat Hanh uses similar ideas in order to explain the concept of 'nondiscrimination' or 'non-duality' ('*advaita*' in Sanskrit) towards others. He says:

> 'One day I was hammering a nail and my right hand was not very accurate and instead of pounding on the nail it pounded on my finger. It put the hammer down and took care of the left hand in a very tender way, as if it were taking care of itself. It did not say, "Left Hand, you have to remember that I have taken good care of you and you have to pay me back in the future." There was no such thinking. And my left hand did not say, "Right Hand, you have done me a lot of harm—give me that hammer, I want justice." My two hands know that they are members of one body; they are in each other.'[175]

---

[175] From his address to the US Congress (2003):
https://plumvillage.org/letters-from-thay/thich-nhat-hanh-address-to-us-congress-september-10-2003/.

On the basis of this, he describes contemporary conflicts, such as that of the Israelis and Palestinians, as stemming from such discriminative thinking, conflicts which would disappear with the realization that both peoples are ultimately 'brothers and sisters...like my two hands.'[176] Just as a limb is an essential part of the body, so is each group of people an essential part of humanity as a whole.

The Community of Humankind

A natural conclusion to the kind of ideas we are discussing is to regard the whole human race as being a kind of 'community of humankind'. Epictetus describes this as follows:

> 'If those things which are said by the philosophers about the common origin of god and men are true, what other alternative is left to men but that which Socrates took, never responding to the one who asked him where he was from with "I am Athenian" or "I am Corinthian" but instead with "I am a citizen of the world".'[177]

Thich Nhat Hanh relates the same message, when discussing the following Vietnamese proverb: 'In order to fight each other, the chicks born from the same mother hen put colors on their faces'.[178] This sentiment indicates that, despite sharing a common humanity, one group of human beings can see themselves as distinct from another to the extent of allowing conflict

---

[176] From his address to the US Congress (2003):
https://plumvillage.org/letters-from-thay/thich-nhat-hanh-address-to-us-congress-september-10-2003/.
[177] *Discourses,* 1.9.1-2.
[178] 1995, 118.

to develop. Thich Nhat Hanh echoes Epictetus above, when he writes:

> 'When will the chicks of the same mother hen remove the colors from their faces and recognize each other as brothers and sisters? The only way to end the danger is for each of us to do so, and to say to others, "I am your brother." "I am your sister." "We are all humankind, and our life is one."'[179]

From all of these ideas, I hope it is clear as to how Buddhist and Stoic concern for our own self will naturally lead us to care for others. As we have seen, this is because neither philosophy regards the self as an isolated entity. Rather, we are connected to others and the rest of the universe in different ways. We are parts of nature and as such also parts of the body of humanity. We are also made up of many elements from outside of ourselves, elements which connect us to the world, others, and nature as a whole. When we have this 'bigger picture' conception of ourselves and truly understand that we are not separate entities, our desire to care for ourselves will naturally extend outwards.

Furtermore, we are social beings and, because of this, when we act out of concern for others, we are automatically benefitted. As Jack Kornfield writes 'Look for any spontaneous thoughts of generosity and follow them. You will find they inevitably make you happy' so too does Marcus Aurelius write 'No one grows tired of receiving benefits, and to bestow benefits is to act according to nature; so never grow tired of receiving

---

[179] 1995, 119.

benefits *by bestowing them on others.*'[180] As a human being, our good is firmly placed in the care of others which, because of the inextricable bonds within all of humanity and the fact that we are inherently social beings, is actually a care of self. In caring for my self, I remember that my 'self' is an inherently social self. In this way, 'selfishness' results, paradoxically, in selflessness.

Turning the Mind Towards Compassion

Both philosophies have analogous mind-trainings aimed at cultivating concern for others on a consistent basis. In Buddhism, this is called *metta* (loving-kindness) practice, and it is aimed at developing good wishes towards all living beings. The practice starts, however, with oneself and *then* extends outwards. The practitioner first repeats inwardly such phrases as these:

> 'May I be held in compassion. May my pain and sorrow be eased. May I be at peace.'[181]

He then replaces 'I' with a loved one, friend, neighbour, a difficult person, an enemy, and '…finally…(with)…the brotherhood and sisterhood of all beings.'[182] In the writings of a Stoic called Hierocles, we find the metaphorical and most similar use of 'concentric circles' as an analogous spiritual exercise. In these circles, one's mind forms the centre, while the next circle stands for one's immediate family, the next for brothers and sisters, the next for aunts and uncles, all

---

[180] *Meditations,* 7.74.
[181] Kornfield (2008), 34.
[182] Kornfield (2008), *34.*

the way to one's city, country and finally the entire human race.[183] The mind-training aspect comes from the Stoic's conscious decision to '...draw the circles together somehow towards the centre, and to keep zealously transferring those from the enclosing circles into the enclosed ones.'[184] In this way, there are noticeable similarities between this Stoic practice and the Buddhist practice of 'metta', or 'loving-kindness' meditation.

The Stoic & Buddhist in Society

> 'The first thing for us to do is to return to ourselves in order to recover ourselves, to be our best....We need to reorganize our daily lives so that we do not allow society to colonize us.'[185] - Thich Nhat Hanh

> 'It is important to withdraw into one's self. Association with a different sort of people unsettles ideas made orderly, reawakens passions, and aggravates mental cankers not yet thoroughly healed. But the two ought to be combined and alternated, some solitude, some society.'[186] - Seneca

Both Stoicism and Buddhism recommend alternating time for oneself and time within society in order not to be overpowered by the latter. Life is about a balance between active engagement and reflection.

For the Stoic or Buddhist, how we interact in our day-to-day living with others is of paramount importance. 'Our daily lives,' writes Thich Nhat Hanh,

---
[183] *Hierocles, from.* Stobaeus 4.671, 7-673, 11 [Long & Sedley, *Hellenistic Philosophers*, 57G].
[184] *Hierocles, from.* Stobaeus 4.671, 7-673, 11 [Long & Sedley, *Hellenistic Philosophers*, 57G].
[185] 1998, 36.
[186] Seneca, *On Tranquillity,* 17.

'the way we drink, what we eat, have to do with the world's political situation.'[187] Furthermore, in Buddhism, the discipline of meditation has in general become increasingly centred on others for it is perceived as a means of understanding and transforming negative qualities within oneself both in order to help others better and to understand the root of humanity's problems on a global level. For Kornfield, meditation is '...not a privilege...but a responsibility,'[188] and, for Thich Nhat Hanh, we meditate not '...to escape from society, but to prepare for reentry into society.'[189] Seeing meditation in this way is described by Batchelor as '...an ethics of empathy to respond to the anguish of a globalized, interdependent world.'[190]

Similarly, Seneca discusses the importance of living well in order to change society at large: 'Our endeavour must be to make our way of life better than the crowd's, not contrary to it; else we shall turn from us and repel the people we wish to improve.'[191] Leading by example, something that is truly in one's control to do, holds positive implications for others. As Seneca writes:

> 'The efforts of a good citizen are never useless; by being heard and seen, by his expression, gesture, silent determination, by his very gait he is of service.'[192]

---

[187] Thich Nhat Hanh (2005a), 77.
[188] Kornfield (1988), 27.
[189] 2005a, 51.
[190] 1997, 112.
[191] Seneca, Letters 5.
[192] Seneca, *On Tranquillity*, 4.

Ultimately, every act, even the smallest one, matters. As the Buddhist says 'Even if I just clap my hands, the effect is everywhere, in the faraway galaxies'[193] so too does the Stoic consider that 'If a single sage at all extends his finger prudently, all the sages throughout the inhabited world are benefited.'[194] There is a ripple effect from all our actions.

For both Buddhism and Stoicism, society at large also contains many worrying aspects, aspects which are reflections of misplaced value-judgements about what truly matters in life. But this fact also means that there is work to be done in making society a better place. In Buddhism, the three mental poisons (greed, hatred and delusion) are not just matters for the individual to overcome. Instead, as Batchelor writes, these drives are '...embodied in the very economic, military, and political structures that influence the lives of the majority of people on earth,'[195] an idea shared by Kornfield when he writes that '...on the global scale, ignorance manifests as injustice, racism, exploitation, and violence.'[196] Likewise, Epictetus notes that there would be no war or oppression without misplaced values:

> '...such are the pitfalls that come to mankind, this is why there exists the siege of cities and their destruction, *whenever correct value-judgements are destroyed*. It is then that women are taken into captivity, then that children are enslaved and the

---

[193] Thich Nhat Hanh (2005a), 9.
[194] Plutarch, *On Stoic Self-Contradictions (De Comm. Not.)* 1086f.
[195] 1997, 112.
[196] 2008, 26.

men themselves slaughtered - are these things not bad?'[197]

The problems we see in a person's own individual mind are merely a microcosm of a much larger human picture. Our inability as humans to sit quietly and observe the workings of our own mind in meditation, with an internal ethical compass, is reflected in the widespread destruction that human beings can bring down upon each other. As such, the Stoic and Buddhist recognise that the kind of path they follow should contribute to an overall force for good in society.

Stoic & Buddhist Care for Others

> 'The Buddha was once asked by a leading disciple, "Would it be true to say that a part of our training is for the development of love and compassion?" The Buddha replied, "No, it would not be true to say this. It would be true to say that the whole of our training is for the development of love and compassion."'[198]

Compassion in Buddhism is of central importance. It revolves primarily around understanding the nature of the other person's suffering. *The Fourth Mindfulness Training* by Thich Nhat Hanh states:

> 'Aware that looking deeply at the nature of suffering can help us develop compassion and find ways out of suffering, we are determined not to avoid or close our eyes before suffering. We are committed to finding ways, including personal contact, images, and sounds, to be with those who suffer, so we can understand their situation deeply and

---

[197] *Discourses,* 1.28.25.
[198] From Feldman (1998), 19.

help them transform their suffering into compassion, peace and joy.'[199]

The Buddhist seeks to be in direct contact with the suffering of another person in order to help them transform that suffering. There is a risk, however, that doing this may lead to becoming overwhelmed by the suffering of others ('compassion fatigue'). In light of this, Thich Nhat Hanh writes of 'Karuna' (the Sanskrit word for 'compassion') as follows:

> 'Karuna is usually translated as "compassion," but that is not exactly correct. "Compassion" is composed of *com* ("together with") and *passion* ("to suffer"). But we do not need to suffer to remove suffering from another person. Doctors, for instance, can relieve their patients' suffering without experiencing the same disease themselves. If we suffer too much, we may be crushed and unable to help.'[200]

The point of compassion for others is to relieve the suffering of the other person and not to be afflicted by that affliction. Epictetus makes a similar point:

> 'Do not hold back from sympathizing with the distressed person in your speech and, if the situation allows it, even to cry with him. But make sure that you do not cry within yourself.'[201]

In this sense, the Stoics and Buddhists profoundly agree. To 'cry within yourself' is to risk being unable to help the other person effectively. Indeed, in Thich Nhat Hanh's definition of compassion 'as the intention and capacity to relieve and transform suffering and lighten

---

[199] From Thich Nhat Hanh (2005a), 93.
[200] 1998, 172.
[201] *Handbook* §16.

sorrows,'[202] we detect Long's assessment of Stoicism that '...the task of a Stoic comforter is not to become upset oneself but to try to assuage the afflicted person.'[203] Concern for others must be linked with some kind of wisdom that allows the comforter to remain strong in herself. In Stoicism, it is very important that our concern for others remains effective. When faced with someone who needs help, we need to remember 'what is up to us' in the situation in question. What actions can we actually take to help the situation (even if that action is just to listen with compassion)? Stoics do not live in their own 'virtuous bubble'. Stoic virtue finds its most active expression in how we treat others and their primary focus is placed on what is actually in our power to do to influence the situation wisely. In this way, Stoicism removes the tendency for unhelpfully overemotional or, conversely, apathetic responses to difficult situations involving the suffering of others.

We are even to try to understand those who harm us. That is not to say that we condone their behaviour, but we try to see what has led that person to act in that way. Marcus Aurelius counsels himself:

> 'Whenever somebody wrongs you, ask yourself at once, 'What conception of good and bad led him to commit such a wrong?' And when you have seen that, you will pity him, and feel neither surprise nor anger.'[204]

This does not just apply to relations we may have with others, but to how we should think of those who have

---

[202] *Handbook* §16.
[203] 2002, 253.
[204] *Meditations,* 7.28.

committed wrongs against society. Both Buddhism and Stoicism have similar positions when it comes to understanding why certain people may break the law, commit wrongs and how to 'rehabilitate' those people. The following two passages by Epictetus and Thich Nhat Hanh illustrate this similarity:

> 'Should not this brigand or adulterer be executed? Certainly not, but you should ask instead 'should not this man who has made a mistake and has been deluded about the most important things and who has been blinded - not in his faculty of vision of things white and black - but in his ability to understand what is right and wrong, should not this man be put to death? And if you put it like that, you will realize how inhumane is the thing which you suggest, and that it is akin to saying 'ought not this blind man, or this deaf man, be put to death?'[205]
>
> - Epictetus

> 'If we look at the death penalty in the light of Interdependent Co-Arising, we see that such an extreme punishment is not reasonable. (...) Of course, it is very difficult to forgive the person who harms us. Our first response is often anger and a desire for revenge. If, however, we are able to look deeply in the light of Interdependent Co-Arising, we may be able to see that if we had grown up, been educated, or experienced life the way that criminal had, we would not be very different from him. When we understand this, we may even begin to feel protective towards him instead of angry or vengeful.'[206]
>
> - Thich Nhat Hanh

---

[205] *Discourses,* 1.18.5-7.
[206] 2006b, 202.

In both philosophies, those who commit crimes are seen as the product of an environment that created them and formed in them misplaced values about what truly matters in life. As such rehabilitation is better than punishment. Epictetus suggests that the solution is to 'show them the error of their ways and you will see how quickly they let go of their wrongdoings'.[207] Indeed, if someone has acted out of ignorance, how can one justify anger as the correct response? Epictetus' analogy of the person ignorant of the good being akin to that of a blind man is apt, for one would not punish a blind man for being unable to see.

And we could so easily have been that 'blind' man, had we been born into his family or suffered what he had suffered. Thich Nhat Hanh came to the following realization when reading of the rape of a young girl by a sea pirate: 'I realized that if I had been born in his village and had lived a similar life - economic, educational, and so on - it is likely that I would now be that sea pirate. So it is not easy to take sides.'[208] To have this kind of compassion is the pinnacle of Buddhist concern for others, even though it demands much of us (and, again, it does not mean that the actions of the person in question are condoned: everyone must take responsibility for their own actions). It involves an understanding of the tragedy of mistaken values, imposed on the individual by a mistaken society, and the tragedy of internalised pain that has gone unloved.

---

[207] *Discourses,* 1.18.4.
[208] 1988, 31.

There is a beautiful poem by Thich Nhat Hanh, 'Please Call Me by My True Names', which encapsulates this compassionate understanding. It serves as a fitting end to this chapter:

> 'I am the child in Uganda, all skin and bones,
> My legs as thin as bamboo sticks.
> And I am the arms merchant,
> Selling deadly weapons to Uganda
>
> I am the twelve-year-old girl,
> refugee on a small boat,
> who throws herself into the ocean
> after being raped by a sea pirate.
> And I am the pirate,
> My heart not yet capable
> Of seeing and loving.
>
> I am a member of the politburo
> With plenty of power in my hands.
> And I am the man who has to pay
> His 'debt of blood' to my people
> Dying slowly in a forced-labor camp.
>
> My joy is like Spring, so warm
> It makes flowers bloom all over the Earth.
> My pain is like a river of tears
> So vast it fills the four oceans.
>
> Please call me by my true names,
> So that I can hear all my cries and laughter at once,
> So I can see that my joy and pain are one.
>
> Please call me by my true names,
> So I can wake up
> And the door of my heart
> Could be left open,
> The door of compassion.'[209]

---

[209] 1999, 72-73.

Conclusion

I hope that this short book has shown that there is considerable similarity between those parts of Stoicism that more and more in the modern world are finding useful and Buddhism as it is so often practiced in the West. At this point, I wish to offer some final reflections on the nature of the ongoing adaptations of Buddhism and of Stoicism and also to consider in what ways each philosophy could learn from the other and, in doing so, I hope to offer helpful reflections for those who may be seeking to practise a combination of both.

Similarities in the Adaptation Process

> 'That many Western Buddhist teachers appear instinctively drawn to the texts that resonate with ideas buried in our own tradition should, in one sense, hardly be surprising. What is surprising though, is that I suspect most of them are not aware of what they are doing.'
>
> Stephen Batchelor (Email Correspondence)

As we have seen earlier, Western Buddhism is highly selective in its use of original Buddhist texts. Only those texts or extracts which explicitly resonate with the highly practical, compassion-oriented nature of Western Buddhism tend to discussed, along with those texts which encourage personal enquiry. You are unlikely to find too many modern-day Buddhists who will read through the Pali Canon, the Buddha's original teachings (contrast this with those who follow 'religions of the book', such as Christianity, who will nearly always primarily seek inspiration from their religion's founding texts). Instead, to be a Buddhist in the West today most often means to read primarily not the Buddha but the wisdom of contemporary Buddhist teachers, even if, as Stephen Batchelor says above, many of those teachers may be unaware of why they chose certain sources over others.

Something similar is perhaps occurring with Stoicism. Although there are many modern Stoics who first and foremost do read the ancient texts, there are also, as Stoicism gains in popularity, an increasing number who primarily read the works of modern writers. Books by Donald Robertson, William Irvine, Massimo Pigluicci, or Ryan Holiday are often the 'go-to' reads for modern Stoics. Most modern writers on Stoicism tend (understandably) to downplay the theistic nature of ancient Stoicism and some may even downplay the central importance of virtue in the philosophy. There could be a risk in this adaptation process that Stoicism, which asks hard-hitting questions about what is truly important in life, could be reduced to something which merely serves us and our pre-existing goals rather than asking us to rethink our goals in the first place.

But, on the other hand, adaptation is a healthy thing and the sign of a living and breathing philosophy. Without adaptation, systems ossify, become rigid, lose their meaning. And both Stoicism and Buddhism, by their very nature, demand to be adapted. Batchelor is right, in my view, to say that the central Buddhist ideas of 'no-self' and of impermanence also apply to Buddhism itself: Buddhism does not have a fixed essence, and is subject to change just as much as the rest of the universe. Similarly, it makes sense that Stoicism too, a philosophy for which impermanence was also a central idea, is requiring of change. Indeed, Stoicism asks of its followers to be active participants in discussing the very fabric of that philosophy. It is worth repeating Seneca's earlier point that 'We are not subjects of a (philosophical) monarch; every individual asserts his freedom'.[210] There is no Stoic Catechism. Stoicism in the ancient world was always engaging in a process of adaptation from its very inception. It changed then and it changes now too.

Given this, as long as there is a tolerance and respect among Stoics for those who either believe or do not believe in the Divine, there should be no need to devalue sincerely worked out efforts to develop a modern, stand-alone form of Stoic ethics. What is abundantly clear too is that the ongoing adaptation of Buddhism *has* worked as an experiment and there is no reason why modern-day Stoics should not engage in a similar, and carefully considered, experiment with Stoicism.

On a related point, there are some areas in which Stoicism sorely needs to be adapted. Indeed, there are some aspects of Stoicism which, in their ancient forms, are, to put it bluntly, positively backward. Although Musonius Rufus, a lesser known Roman Stoic, regarded that women were equally capable of virtue as men,[211]

---

[210] Seneca, *Letters 33.4.*
[211] Musonius Rufus, *Discourses* 3.

Epictetus, for example, thought that women were the 'common property' of men in the same way that a roast pig is the 'common property' of all those at a feast.[212] Modern accounts of the inherently 'progressive' nature of Stoicism tend to focus on the former example and not, unsurprisingly, the latter. Similarly, Musonius Rufus considered sexual relations between men to be 'a monstrous thing and contrary to nature.'[213] In ancient Stoicism, slaves could be 'free' in the philosophical sense of the word but no Stoic ever questioned the validity of the concept of slavery, from a legal perspective. These are issues in the ancient texts that modern Stoics, rather then claiming that their philosophy is inherently enlightened and progressive, need to look closely at and deal with the fact that, in its ancient form, Stoicism, while containing certain 'prototypes' for equality, did also operate on the basis of a conception of 'Nature' that goes against much modern thinking on what is right, fair and equal. In the same way that modern Buddhism has had to extend its compassion to diverse groups of people so as to become inherently inclusive, so too does Stoicism need to engage with its own texts critically so as to ensure that it too can be fully inclusive.

The 'Silicon Valley' Stoic

There is one major risk that may occur, and which is arguably already occurring, in the ongoing adaptation of Stoicism. And that risk is that virtue may get left out. That is to say that, if Stoicism no longer becomes about

---

[212] Epictetus, *Discourses* 2.4.
[213] Musonius Rufus, *Discourses* 12.

rethinking our top priorities in life, then it could just become reduced to techniques and 'coffee-mug' quotations of advice. While these can be helpful, and there is nothing wrong with them in and of themselves, it would be a mistake to think of applying such techniques or quotations as 'Stoicism'. In line with this, there is an increasing risk at the moment of what could be called the 'Silicon Valley Stoic', someone who uses Stoic techniques and ideas not to rethink his priorities about what constitutes a good life, but instead to become the 'best entrepreneur' he can be, using Stoic techniques and ideas only in so far as they can help him to achieve that aim. There is a risk that Stoic ideas and techniques may end up becoming subservient to the profit line. I have noticed that some driven workaholics tend to be attracted to Stoicism, and they misunderstand it in such a way that they reinforce and validate a way of life which is deeply unphilosophical. The same is happening with meditation. There are business executives who meditate not so as to learn about and heal their own inner suffering but so as to become 'more productive'. They then might expect their employees to practise mindfulness for the same reason. There is a risk that the same could happen with Stoicism: be Stoic so as to be a greater and more productive 'economic unit'.

On the other hand, it need not always carry risks to leave out virtue. For example, I do think that taking certain aspects of Stoicism, including techniques and key ideas, and reframing those to be appropriate in a more general therapeutic context, is a good idea. By this I mean that, in the same way that Buddhist meditation techniques were adapted to form the Mindfulness Based Stress Reduction (MBSR) course, an eight-week program of mindfulness meditation, so too could something similar occur with Stoicism. The resulting program, which might focus on resilience, need not mention Stoicism explicitly, in the same way that the MBSR course does not focus explicitly on Buddhism.

Combining Stoicism and Buddhism: How Can Each Philosophy Learn From the Other?

There are real strengths to both Stoicism and Buddhism. Both provide well-thought out and realistic antidotes to a world of 'overly optimistic' psychological self-help. Both Stoicism and Buddhism aim to encourage a flourishing life within a realistic conception of it. Furthermore, both are philosophies which try, for the most part, to apply to *all* aspects of how we live. This is refreshing in an age where psychological advice tends to apply just to particular problems. How do I quit smoking? How can I reduce my anxiety in social situations or my perfectionism? Of course, it is very helpful to have specific techniques and answers to specific problems, and this can be life changing, but nowadays we often miss 'bigger picture' approaches which can reframe our life as a whole, including all, or at least most, of the specific problems within it.

But in what ways can Stoicism inform Buddhism and vice versa?

One way that stands out immediately is the practice of meditation. In particular, the ability to learn to observe thoughts and feelings from a slight distance, as one does in Buddhist meditation, would be very helpful for applying Stoic ethics in the moment more skillfully. Greater self-awareness from the practice of meditation would allow someone more easily to take a step back and ask the key Stoic question: 'what is "up to me" in this moment?' Also, there is a certain restfulness of mind that the Buddhist practice of meditation could bring to Stoicism which could only be beneficial.

But there is a much more impactful way in which I believe both philosophies could inform each other, and this requires some explanation.

My sense is that Stoicism's strength is to be found in providing an 'ethical framework' by which to live our lives, an internal reference point to which we can refer when faced with life's problems. Asking ourselves 'which ethical qualities will allow me to meet this current situation best of all?' is a question that can help reframe some of life's greatest challenges.

However, what Stoicism can lack at times is a more compassionate and heartfelt response to life's difficulties and tragedies. 'Heart' and 'compassion' are terms you will find regularly in Western Buddhism but you would be hard-placed to find something equivalent in the ancient Stoic writings (and the modern ones too). Modern Buddhists are not afraid to approach emotions, even the most overwhelming ones, with compassionate awareness whereas the Stoics, as it seems to me, are more interested in immediately 'reframing' more 'difficult' emotions by working out an ethical response that can dampen the effect of the emotion while finding the most productive response to the situation. But emotions, even though they may not live up to Stoic standards of 'wisdom', are, if considered closely enough, often the result of very understandable previous life experiences (particularly from childhood) and they are deserving of our love and understanding *just as they are.* The Stoic true to his philosophy would disagree with this. In Stoicism, there is no time for loving or understanding with compassion one's own feelings just as they are: the emphasis instead is placed on changing the emotion in a wiser direction as soon as possible.

But is it so wise always to seek to change or manipulate ourselves? Sometimes, the most helpful shifts can occur just from letting our emotional experience be, with a gently observant love. Such change when it occurs in this way is intrinsic, from an innate wisdom, and it arises from self-trust and learning that, actually, even the most difficult emotions, if attended to with love, can transform in wholesome directions *by themselves.*

In this way, Stoicism strikes me as a more paternal philosophy, Buddhism as a more maternal one. Stoicism seeks to change the individual with a firm but wise hand. Buddhism (in many of its Western forms, at least) seeks to change the person by first letting them be exactly as they are, and letting a loving acceptance of experience itself be the teacher.

However, we need a balance between paternal and maternal wisdom in our lives. Buddhism's focus, particularly thanks to the emphasis on mindfulness, is continuously placed on a gently loving acceptance of the present moment. In having this focus, though, we might tend to miss the 'bigger picture' of what our lives are about and what kind of 'ethical project' we are engaging in longer-term. The Stoics are at their best when they offer us their examinations of the misplaced values of society at large and why it is that virtue is the most important thing, the thing which fulfills our human nature, especially when it is combined with actions that are beneficial to others. We are social creatures and virtue accordingly needs to have a social dimension in order truly to fulfill us. Such ideas can provide an ethical framework for our life, and this sort of framework, or 'bigger picture' conception of what life is about, could helpfully be a part of Western Buddhism.

One way to link these philosophies together would be to add compassion, love and acceptance to the traditional Stoic virtues. In other words, one could add those more loving and maternal qualities to the Stoic ethical system such that, when a Stoic asks herself, 'what is "up to me" in this current situation?', compassion, love and acceptance would be as valid answers as fortitude, courage, moderation, justice, and other Stoic ethical qualities. Similarly, the Buddhist could add to his philosophy the practice of values-clarification. By asking himself bigger questions such as 'What constitutes a life-well lived?', 'What really matters in the end?' or 'What is the best use of time?', the Buddhist could develop an internal set of well-worked out and steadfast ethical beliefs on which to draw upon throughout his life.

In these ways, 'Behaviourism towards virtue' could be combined with 'Behaviourism with heart'. We need both an idea of what ethical values will get us through life along with a way of lovingly accepting the emotional flow of the journey. A combination of Stoicism and Buddhism could provide just that.

Final words

Buddhism and Stoicism are paths which go 'against the stream' of what society expects of us, and, for this reason, they are also often lonely paths. The answers are not all set out in advance to be accepted blindly. They challenge us and require us to be very active participants in understanding and responding to life's greatest challenges and existential questions. The Buddha's suggestion to seek no other refuge than oneself and to train oneself well,[214] is paralleled in Marcus' advice to himself 'to be upright, rather than be set upright'.[215] This seems hard, and it is. It was counter-cultural at the time and it is counter-cultural now.

But that we can do it is never doubted.

I shall end this book with words first from Jack Kornfield and then Epictetus which require no further analysis:

> 'Our belief in a limited and impoverished identity is such a strong habit that without it we are afraid we wouldn't know how to be. If we fully acknowledged our dignity, it could lead to radical life changes. It could ask something huge of us.'[216]

> 'As it is necessary that each and every man relates to each thing as a result of the opinion he has of it,

---
[214] *Dhammapada*, 160.
[215] *Meditations*, 7.12.
[216] 2008, 12.

then those few people, who believe that they are born for fidelity, modesty and to certainty in how they use their own mind, they think nothing base or ignoble about themselves. As for everyone else, the exact opposite is the case.'[217]

---

[217] 1.3.4-5.

Bibliography

Primary

Batchelor S., *Buddhism Without Beliefs* (Bloomsbury, 1997).

———— *Canonical Citations: Source Texts for a Secular Buddhism* (Ongoing, see Media Bibliography).

———— *Confession of a Buddhist Atheist* (Spiegel & Grau, 2011a).

———— *The Awakening of the West* (Echo Points Books, 2011b).

Epictetus, *Discourses & Encheiridion*, Loeb Ed. (tr. Oldfather, 1998).

Feldman, C., 'Nurturing Compassion', in Eppsteiner, F. (ed)., *The Path of Compassion: Writings on Socially Engaged in Buddhism* (Buddhist Peace Fellowship, 1988), 19-23.

Gunaratana, B., *Mindfulness in Plain English* (Wisdom Publications, 2002,).

Hierocles, *Elements of Ethics: Fragments, and Excerpts*, tr. Ilaria Ramelli (Society of Biblical Literature, 2009).

Kornfield, J., *Bringing Home the Dharma*: *Awakening Right Where You Are* (Shambala, 2011).

———— 'The Path of Compassion,' in Eppsteiner, F. (ed)., *The Path of Compassion: Writings on Socially Engaged in Buddhism* (Buddhist Peace Fellowship, 1988), 24-30.

———— *The Wise Heart: Buddhist Psychology for the West* (Ebury Publishing, 2008,).

Laertius Diogenes, *The Life of Zeno* [Perseus Online Library].

Marcus Aurelius, *Meditations*, tr. Hard R., introd. Gill C., (Oxford, 2011,).

———— Loeb Ed. (tr. C.R. Haines), 1930.

Seneca, *Selected Essays and Letters*, tr. Moses Hades (Norton Library, 1968).

Thich-Nhat-Hanh, 'Please Call Me by My True Names', in Eppsteiner, F. (ed)., *The Path of Compassion: Writings on Socially Engaged in Buddhism* (Buddhist Peace Fellowship, 1988), 31-39.

———— 'The Individual, Society and Nature', in Eppsteiner, F. (ed)., *The Path of Compassion: Writings on Socially Engaged in Buddhism* (Buddhist Peace Fellowship, 1988,), 40-46.

———— *A Basket of Plums* (Parallax Press, 2009).

———— *Being Peace* (Parallax Press, 2005a).

———— *Call Me by My True Names: Collected Poems* (Parallax Press, 1999).

———— *Living Buddha, Living Christ* (Rider, 2005b).

———— *Peace is Every Step: The Path of Mindfulness in Everyday Life* (Rider, 1995)

———— *Present Moment Wonderful Moment: Mindfulness Verses for Everyday Living* (Parallax Press, 2006c).

———— *The Heart of the Buddha's Teachings* (Rider, 1998).

———— *The Miracle of Mindfulness* (Beacon Press, 1975).

———— *Transformation and Healing: Sutra on the Four Establishments of Mindfulness* (Parallax Press, 2006a).

———— *Understanding Our Mind* (Parallax Press, 2006b).

Resources for Original Buddhist Texts

Dhammapada, The, tr. Max Müller, (Watkins, 2006).

Pali Buddhist Texts, tr. Johansson R., (Routledge, 1998).

Secondary

Chappell, D., 'Buddhist Responses to Religious Pluralism: What are the Ethical Issues?', in Wei-hsun Fu, C. & Wawrytko, S. (eds.), *Buddhist Ethics and Modern Society* (Greenwood, 1991), 355-370.

Dobbin R., *Epictetus: Discourse Book 1*, (Clarendon, 2011).

Gill, C., *The Structured Self in Hellenistic and Roman Thought* (OUP, 2006).

Gill, C., *Meditations 1-6: Introduction, Translation and Commentary* (Clarendon, forthcomingA).

Gill, C., 'Antiochus' Theory of oikeiōsis' (forthcomingB).

Hadot P., *Philosophy as a Way of Life* (Blackwell, 2011).

Johns, *The Present Moment in Later Stoicism* (forthcoming article).

Keown, D., *Buddhist Ethics: A Very Short Introduction*, (Oxford, 2005).

King, R., *Thomas Merton and Thich Nhat Hanh: Engaged Spirtuality in an Age of Globalization* (Continuum, 2001).

Kitterman in Storhoff G. & Whalen-Bridge, J. (eds.), *American Buddhism as a Way of Life* (State University of New York, 2010).

Lancaster, 'Buddhism and the Contemporary World: The Problem of Social Action in an Urban Environment', in Wei-hsun Fu, C. & Wawrytko, S. (eds.), *Buddhist Ethics and Modern Society* (Greenwood, 1991), 347-354.

Long, A.A., *Epictetus: A Stoic and Socratic Guide to Life* (Oxford, 2002).

McMahan, D., *The Making of Buddhist Modernism* (OUP, 2008).

Nussbaum, M., *The Therapy of Desire* (Princeton, 1996).

Premasiri, P., 'The relevance of the Noble Eightfold Path to Contemporary Society', in Wei-hsun Fu, C. & Wawrytko, S. (eds.), *Buddhist Ethics and Modern Society* (Greenwood, 1991), 131-142.

Purser, R., 'The Myth of the Present Moment', in Mindfulness (2015), 6: 680 (https://link.springer.com/article/10.1007/s12671-014-0333-z).

Robertson, D., *The Philosophy of Cognitive Behavioural Therapy (CBT): Stoic Philosophy as Rational and Cognitive Psychotherapy*, (Karnac, 2010).

Sellars J., *The Art of Living* (Bristol, 2009).

Stephens, W., *Stoic Ethics: Epictetus and Happiness as Freedom* (Continuum, 2007).

Stevenson, *Tradition and Change in the* Sangha*: A Buddhist Historian Looks at Buddhism in America*, in Wei-hsun Fu, C. & Wawrytko, S. (eds.), *Buddhist Ethics and Modern Society* (Greenwood, 1991), 247-258.

Storhoff G. & Whalen-Bridge, J. (eds), *American Buddhism as a Way of Life* (State University of New York, 2010).

Ussher, P., *Stoicism Today: Selected Writings*, Vol. 1 (2014).

Ussher, P., *Stoicism Today: Selected Writings*, Vol. 2 (2016).

Media

Batchelor, *Canonical Citations: Source Texts for a Secular Buddhism* (Ongoing).
[http://www.stephenbatchelor.org/media/Stephen/PDF/Stephen_Batchelor-Pali_Canon-Website-02-2012.pdf]

Ferraiolo, W., 'Roman Buddha' in *Western Buddhist Review*, vol. 5.
[http://www.westernbuddhistreview.com/vol5/index.html]

Gombrich, R., *Stoicism and Buddhism* (Lecture, 2010).
[http://www.ocbs.org/news-ocbsmain-88/105-reflecting-on-my-lecture-buddhism-and-stoicism-a-comparison].

Rosi, M., 'Bouddhisme et Stoïcisme' (2005).
[http://www.zen-occidental.net/pdf/rosi1.pdf]

Thanissaro Bhikku, *The Roots of Buddhist Romanticism* (2012).
[http://www.accesstoinsight.org/lib/authors/thanissaro/rootsofbuddhistromanticism.html]

Other Hyperlinks

Thich-Nhat-Hanh's Interview on Impermanence - http://dharmagates.org/long_live_impermanence.html

BBC report on Thich-Nhat-Hanh and Status of Exile in Vietnam - http://news.bbc.co.uk/1/hi/world/asia-pacific/8278336.stm

Interview with Albert Ellis by Jules Evans on Origins of C.B.T. - http://philosophyforlife.org/albert-ellis-on-philosophy-as-therapy/

Thich-Nhat-Hanh's speech to U.S. Congress - https://plumvillage.org/letters-from-thay/thich-nhat-hanh-address-to-us-congress-september-10-2003/

www.ingramcontent.com/pod-product-compliance
Lightning Source LLC
Chambersburg PA
CBHW051953290426
44110CB00015B/2221